W9-AZB-099

DATE			

THE
MEASURE
OF A
MOUNTAIN

THE MEASURE OF A MOUNTAIN

Beauty and Terror on Mount Rainier

BRUCE BARCOTT

SASQUATCH BOOKS
SEATTLE

Printed in the United States of America.
Distributed in Canada by Raincoast Books Ltd.
01 00 99 98 97   5 4 3 2 1

Portions of this book appeared previously in *Harper's* and *Seattle Weekly*.

Cover design: Karen Schober
Cover/interior photograph: Josef Scaylea
Interior design and composition: Kate Basart
Map: Rolf Goetzinger
Copy editor: Phyllis Hatfield

Library of Congress Cataloging in Publication Data
Barcott, Bruce, 1966–
        The measure of a mountain : beauty and terror on Mount Rainier /
    Bruce Barcott.
                p.   cm.
        Includes bibliographical references (p.   ) and index.
        ISBN 1-57061-074-6
        1. Rainier, Mount (Wash.)—Description and travel. 2. Barcott,
    Bruce, 1966– —Journeys—Washington (State)—Rainier, Mount.
    I. Title.
    F897.R2B23 1997
    917.97'7820443—dc21   97-22029

SASQUATCH BOOKS
615 Second Avenue
Seattle, Washington 98104
(206) 467-4300
books@sasquatchbooks.com
http://www.sasquatchbooks.com

*Sasquatch Books publishes high-quality adult nonfiction and children's books
related to the Northwest (Alaska to San Francisco). For more information about
our titles, contact us at the address above, or view our site on the World Wide Web.*

For my father

CONTENTS

MOUNT RAINIER

THE MOUNTAIN IS OUT

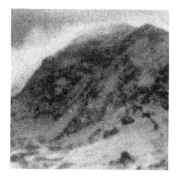

When it rises like a misshapen moon over downtown Seattle, the mountain entrances me, arrests my attention, and rouses my imagination; it makes me weave on wet highways.

On early mornings Rainier wakes above siesta-rate motels on Highway 99, above the waterfront's dromedary cranes and the grey dimple of the Kingdome, above the Space Needle and the Columbia Tower and Tokyo-bound 747s and everything that lives and everything that doesn't, as far as the eye can see. Rainier wakes higher than most of the air we breathe. The sight of it has nearly killed me. More than once its spell has been broken by the headlights of an oncoming car bearing down on my southbound self speeding along the north-bound lane. The mountain never appears in the same place with the same face twice. It possesses a Cheshire talent for appearing and dis-appearing at will. From the highest hill it may lie shrouded in mist, only to show itself an hour later from the middle of Puget Sound. People who have lived in the Pacific Northwest all their lives still stop and stare when Rainier reveals itself. The moment crackles with the thrill of Nature being caught unaware, like seeing an eagle snatch a sockeye from the Sound. On clear winter days the Olympic and Cas-cade mountains flank the trough of Puget Sound like a fence of white-capped waves. We've got mountains like Iowa's got flat. And yet the local vernacular admits only one "Mountain," and when Rainier rises we tell each other, "The Mountain is out." Mount Rainier is at once the most public symbol of the Pacific Northwest and its most sacred pri-vate icon. A friend once disclosed that she says a prayer whenever she sees it. A stranger I met on its high southern flank told me, "You must love this mountain as much as I do," but his reverent tone of voice told me I couldn't. Lou Whittaker, who has climbed Rainier more than one hundred fifty times, told me about returning home from a Himalayan expedition and catching sight of the mountain and feeling it snap his breath clean away.

Like rain and rivers and trees, the mountain is a continuous pres-ence in our lives, but in our psychological landscape it occupies a place separate and greater than the forests and falling water. We look at Rainier and feel love for a mountain, if such a thing is possible. The mountain inspires in us a feeling akin to spiritual awe: reverence, ado-ration, humility. We look at Rainier and regard the vastness of God; yet we look at it and claim it as our own. This strange relationship we have with the mountain is romantic, uninformed, even presumptuous. Rainier is a mountain few of us know.

Mount Rainier is the largest and most dangerous volcano in the United States of America. Its summit reaches 14,410 feet above the sea, and though it was once thought to be the highest point in the nation, now we know better. Outside of Alaska, the four mountains higher than Rainier are Mount Whitney (elevation 14,494 feet), in California's Sierra Nevada range, and Mount Elbert (14,433), Mount Massive (14,421), and Mount Harvard (14,420), in the Sawatch Range of the Rockies. Mount Rainier is more spectacular than all of them. A man who saw it in 1910 wrote: "It is an inspiration and yet a riddle to all who are drawn to the mysterious or who love the sublime." More than two million people visit Rainier every year. Ten thousand try to climb it, and a little more than half of them succeed. The mountain rises 10,000 feet from its base and holds as much snow and ice as the twelve other Cascade volcanoes combined. Its massive ice flows and furious winds so closely mimic Himalayan conditions that the first American climbers to conquer Mount Everest trained on Rainier before leaving for Nepal. Spread an inch thick, its glacial ice would cover the state of Tennessee. A Seattle rock band once wrote a song about Rainier that predicted "It's gonna bloww-wo-wo-wo," but when I asked a geologist, he said it wasn't waiting to explode so much as fall to pieces. Very big pieces.

On a clear morning the mountain can be seen from Canada to Oregon, from the San Juan Islands to Spokane. On cloudy afternoons its form remains visible on personal checks, decorative porcelain, framed postcards, bottled water, billboard ads, and the license plate of every vehicle registered in the state of Washington. Paper placemats printed with maps of the USA—the ones at restaurants where they bring you crayons with the menu—often depict a cartoon salmon jumping over Mount Rainier in Washington state.

I wanted to know more about it. I started cutting work to drive to the mountain. I bought a beater station wagon so I could stay there days at a time and sleep in the back. A couple of times I forgot my sleeping bag and nearly froze to death. I fell asleep to the sound of rain like typewriters on the roof and woke to deer browsing at the fender, and almost hit a twelve-point elk that would have mashed the wagon like yesterday's spuds.

When I had money I stayed in National Park campgrounds and when I didn't I parked on logging roads and hoped the truckers slept in later than I did. I ate in mountain towns—Scaleburgers in Elbe, four-dollar chicken at the Highlander in Ashford—and shared pitchers of Rainier Beer with men who'd lived thirty years without seeing Seattle and hoped to go another thirty before a first encounter.

I carted a library in the back seat and read Dee Molenaar's *The Challenge of Rainier*, Aubrey Haines's *Mountain Fever*, and Edmond Meany's *Mount Rainier: A Record of Exploration*, by the moth-flicker of a fluorescent lantern. I consumed field guides to birds, plants, rocks, and weather. I tried to read Thomas Mann's *The Magic Mountain*, but got so sick of Hans Castorp's anemia that I tossed him in the fire before he had a chance to recover. I got to the end of *The Seven Storey Mountain* before I figured out that Thomas Merton was more interested in monasteries than actual mountains.

I picked the mountain apart bit by bit. My curiosity intruded upon geologists, volcanologists, glaciologists, entomologists, botanists, wildlife biologists, and a large-animal toxicologist in Utah. I talked with priests, monks, and New Age healers. I walked with park rangers and mountain guides. I took to driving around Mount Rainier, always looking for a new way to understand it. When I couldn't stand to sleep in the car anymore, I began walking around the mountain clockwise like a pilgrim. After a year of circumnavigation I went higher, to the climbing camps nearly two miles in the sky. And when that wasn't enough, I walked higher still, pursuing the moment when I would know the mountain as perfectly as myself.

I kept wishing I had a good reason to go to the mountain, but the truth is I didn't. In a perfect narrative world, the woman I loved would have left me and I'd have run into the hills seeking the consolation of wild things. As it happened she waited until the mountain sickness had me in full fever before telling me she couldn't take it anymore. One day at the trailhead she said, "We've got to talk," and ten minutes later we had talked. I stayed up that night watching infomercials and an old Gary Cooper movie and considered moving to Montana. By morning I had ruled out Montana. I decided to quit my job and pursue whatever it was I was pursuing at Mount Rainier. Now I had the time.

Over Christmas dinner I promised my grandmother I would never go to the mountain alone. I spent the next two years breaking my word. I walked alone above the Emmons Glacier and watched the sun turn its ice nine shades of blue. I walked alone through the Ohanapecosh forest where lichen the color of cucumber meat dripped from absinthe cedar boughs, and sword ferns and maidenhair ferns and bracken and salal grew out of a carpet of clubfoot moss, and the light dappled through so many emerald filters that I felt I had landed on the planet Green. I walked alone to glacier snouts and waterfalls and mining camps and snowfields. I walked alone into lakes so cold they made my veins pop out like licorice.

There is something extraordinary about being alone on a mountain. Vulnerability sharpens every sense. Fear visits the body with a physical coldness. Moments of bliss are intensified and made melancholy by the realization that the moment will be yours alone and never shared. Only solo do you understand the indiscriminate power of the mountain and feel to your humble bones the insignificance of a human voice raised upon it.

Mount Rainier is on the North American continent, in the United States of America, in the state of Washington, in the southeastern corner of Pierce County, sixty miles from Seattle but a two-hour drive because the roads are so twisty. In 1899 the federal government established 235,000 acres around the mountain as the nation's fifth national park, an action the chief benefit of which, a century later, turned out to be the protection of the area's billions of square feet of old-growth timber. Over the years engineers have dreamed of building a road encircling the mountain, but it has never been done; high mountains are one of the few geographic entities through which engineers can't blast and pave.

Mount Rainier National Park's most popular destination is Paradise, a 5,400-foot-high alpine meadow that overlooks the Nisqually Glacier and upon which sits an architectural abomination of a visitor center, a wood-and-cement spaceship that landed in the mid-sixties. Paradise was named in 1885 by Virinda Longmire, wife of the mountain's first white settler and namesake of the site of the National Park Inn a few miles below Paradise, who rode a horse to the high meadow and exclaimed, "O, what a paradise!" The nearest thing to a town around Mount Rainier is Ashford, population 600, whose points of interest include P.J.'s Unique Boutique, Mierke's Mobile Home Park, the Highlander Tavern, the Ashford Country Store ("Since 1905"), and Whittaker's Bunkhouse, where Lou will chat with you on his coffee break before getting back up to fix the roof. If you leave Ashford to go deeper into the backwoods, you get into real *Deliverance* country. My mother, a Pierce County librarian, sometimes works bookmobile runs in mountain towns where patrons browse the shelves while their animals wait outside. And I'm not talking about cats and dogs.

I had as much business going into the mountain as I had harpooning my own whale. My experience on mountains was limited to groomed ski trails except for a sojourn across a precipitous ridge on Alaska's modest Mount Alyeska with my parents and my sister in the early seventies. The harrowing memory of that trek is forever seared into my brain. I'm just no good with heights. Chairlifts scare the devil out of me. I shrink from the edges of sharp cliffs. Recently I climbed a peak in the Tatoosh Mountains directly south of Mount Rainier. At the very top, where the rock dropped away two hundred feet, my partner bounded across the apex while I dropped to all fours and stuck to terra firma like a limpet.

Despite my acrophobic tendencies, I was determined to encounter the mountain up close. I joined the ranks of the REI Army, that legion of gear-obsessed soldiers who suit up every weekend and drive into the hills to hunt down and kill their God-given portion of wilderness transcendence. Enlistment began with the purchase of a five-hundred-dollar Gore-Tex jacket and rain pants at Recreational Equipment Incorporated (REI), the outdoor goods cooperative whose funky Capitol Hill store sucked every ounce of fat out of my slender paycheck. REI considers its mission the celebration and conservation of the great outdoors, but I couldn't help feeling cowed every time I stepped through its doors. Beneath the happy-face of local outdoor culture there lurked a possessive territoriality that kept outsiders out and insiders in. At REI a humorless sense of moral superiority seemed de rigueur, fostered by the belief that those who stomp the natural world under their Vibram soles are healing Gaea, while the rest of the world tears her asunder.

In this world I was a rank outsider. During the equipment sales that turned REI into a bedlam of beards and fleece, the company offered discounts to the customer with the lowest co-op number. Few baubles in the Northwest command such instant respect as a low-numbered REI card. The co-op's membership began with No. 1 in 1938 and now runs into the low four millions. Jim Whittaker, the first American to climb Mount Everest, is No. 647. I am No. 3,538,286. I bear the shame every day of my life.

I asked a friend who had hiked across Spain for advice on equipment. He told me to buy the best backpack I could find. Spare no expense. So I visited McHale & Company, a custom backpack shop that outfitted many of Seattle's world-class mountaineers. Dan McHale, an intense climber with the compact body of a wrestler, made the gear in his shop near Seattle's Fremont Bridge and tested it on summit runs up Rainier and other Cascade peaks. His customers were on intimate terms with K2 and Everest.

Dan McHale was not thrilled to see my bespectacled visage darken his door. He came out from behind the shop counter to see if he could direct me to wherever it was I really wanted to be, whereupon I announced that I intended to encircle Mount Rainier and was shopping for a pack that was up to the challenge. He sized me up in a word—*novice*—that he had the tact not to spit at me, then began filling one of his high-tech rucks with every object of weight within reach. Dumbbells, sleeping bags, boulders, tents. After adjusting a half-dozen straps, he let me go. I stumbled, regained my balance, and stood with my legs scissored for structural support. The act of not toppling strained every muscle in my body. "Take a walk around, see how it feels," McHale told me, before retreating to his shop. I took three steps, turned, and squatted like a nineteenth-century gymnast. I repeated the routine, desperate to look as if I knew what I was doing. *Weight feels good there. Excellent lumbar support.* I began to perspire. McHale peeked around the corner and eyed me as if I had disrobed.

"Um . . . why don't you try it *outside*?"

After a toilsome stroll around the block, I told McHale it felt terrific. "Yeah," he said. "You go to REI, some kid will tell you his pack will adjust to your height, but"—let me add that I'm six feet four and thin as a stork—"this one is designed for a frame like yours." I asked how much it would cost.

"I'd fit you in a standard-size pack, which usually starts at about five-and-a-quarter."

Perhaps he misheard. " . . . pounds?"

"Five hundred twenty-five dollars."

Oh.

At REI some kid told me his pack would adjust to my height, and it more or less did, and I bought a purple-and-black backpack whose model name I hoped would eventually match the attitude of its owner: The Renegade. At six pounds ten ounces The Renegade boasted forty-eight hundred cubic inches of interior space, and though I had no idea what that meant, the phrase "forty-eight hundred cubic inches" sounded impressive and powerful in the way that "dual exhaust and twin over-head cams" does. A buyer's guide mentioned The Renegade's excellent load-channeling and weight-transferring abilities, but it needn't have bothered. I was sold on the name alone.

I also purchased a pair of boots that were, I think, made in Germany, because they were called "der Wanderschuhe." Der Wanderschuhe hurt der feet, so I broke in the stiff leather by rubbing waterproofing wax into them and walking around town. Since I live in Seattle near the Space Needle, my hiking is often limited to concrete trails. I strolled to the waterfront and watched a couple of guys who spoke Spanish reel a rock cod out of the junkwater of Elliott Bay, and ate some fish and chips at Ivar's, and continued south to the Kingdome, where my father works. I showed off my boots and told him I was going to hike around Mount Rainier, to which he replied, "Why don't we climb it?" and I thought, Uh-oh.

When I walked home I raised a blister and my boots squeaked.

START WALKING

The sound of mountain rain provided no comfort. The skin of my tent spattered and popped with the drool of the western sky. Earlier in the day the forest's thick hemlock canopy had sheltered me from all but a fine mist, but now the saturated trees passed the rain straight to the bracken, salal, and me down here in the understory.

It had rained all day and would continue through the night. At midnight I pulled on wool socks and a damp watch cap. At two a.m. I switched on my headlamp to check the time, which is what you do when it's the middle of the night and you can't sleep for the sound of your own teeth chattering and you wonder how many more hours you must endure. I shivered and fetaled into my sleeping bag, pulling the drawstring so tight that sight remained the only sense available to the world. This was what it meant to be in the wilderness: cold, wet, and alone.

Falling water has always been a healing balm when I find myself with a despairing mind and cracking soul. The winter rains of Puget Sound, which never start and stop but only drizzle on, signal the cool comfort of home. Walking Seattle's downtown streets on the first misty morning of autumn fills me with a delight similar to what northern Alaskans feel when the sun returns after months of winter darkness. Rain is my assurance that life will go on. But not up here. Rain is the mountain's primal foe, breaking and grinding and flushing away the very body of Rainier. Water has always been the mountain's enemy; now it had become mine. First night on the mountain, first lesson: Expect discomfort.

With der Wanderschuhe broken in and The Renegade fat with fifty pounds of food and gear, I had set out to circumnavigate Mount Rainier. It was early September, a time when summer and fall still wrestled for dominion. My route would take me from Longmire, low on the mountain's southwestern flank, north to Lake Mowich; then I'd turn east towards the visitor center known as Sunrise, fall south to the lush forests of Ohanapecosh, and cut across the southern section to Longmire. Round trip, ninety-two miles. If all went well I'd return to Longmire in twelve days. The route was called the Wonderland Trail, which struck me as too Pollyannish by half. "If there is one thing that those who have done the Wonderland would wish to convey to future hikers," wrote trail veteran Bette Filley, "it is to be psychologically prepared. It's a *tough* trail." With naive bravado I had booked a room at the Longmire National Park Inn twelve days hence, when I planned to stride into the dining room, grizzled as a prospector, throw my pack on the table, and demand a bottle of champagne and the thickest steak in the house. Anyone can dream.

Things went wrong from the start. The night before I set out, my father and I ferried my equipment south in his pickup. A heavy rain opened up as we drove down Interstate 5 listening to Dave Niehaus talk the Mariners through a loss to the Orioles. We sat like hillbillies watching the wipers slap when it occurred to me that we were riding in a truck with an—*Oh Christ!*—open bed. We had forgotten to cover it with a tarp. "GET OFF! THE FREEWAY! NOW!" I said, mustering enormous restraint to keep myself from yanking the wheel from my father's hands. By the time I pulled it from the flatbed, The Renegade had gained two pounds of liquid weight.

The next morning I joined the trail, my spirit nearly broken with fright. The dampness of The Renegade pressed against my back. The buckle that snugged the pack to my chest and performed some unknown but doubtlessly crucial function in The Renegade's acclaimed load-channeling operation had disappeared in the open-bed truck fiasco. Twenty minutes into the trail the clouds knit together and wept. By nightfall everything except my sleeping bag had accepted the cold weight of water.

That night I tossed between fear and failure. I had two choices: Admit defeat and turn back, preserving life and abandoning dignity, pride, and honor; or press on into a mountain storm without a partner, experience, competence, or a phone to call the Tacoma Mountain Rescue squad. My notebook still held the promise of crisp, trim pages. During the night I flipped it open and registered my situation. "Pissing rain. Wet everywhere. Misery." A few hours later, at the high tide of vinegar, I recorded a final assessment: "This sucks big wang."

The morning arrived with sound, not light. A bird flew over my tent, and from the sound of it the thing had beaten wind straight out of *Jason and the Argonauts. Fwuff fwuff fwuff.* The sound of a Persian carpet being shaken. I could practically feel the air compress beneath its wings. I peeked out in time to see it clamp onto the bicep of a cedar twenty yards away. Furry and black, it let out a guttural *awwk-grawwk* to which every town crow aspires: Raven.

"A very intelligent bird, the Common Raven seems to apply reasoning in situations entirely new to it," writes Miklos Udvardy in the *National Audubon Society Field Guide to North American Birds.* "Its 'insight' behavior is comparable to that of a dog." Comparable to that of a coyote, actually. Raven and Coyote are the great protagonists of Pacific Northwest Native American mythology. They are the heroes and goats, tricksters and fools who prepare the world for the coming of the people. When I lived in Alaska as a child, my mother sent my sister and me trudging over the snow to the Sand Lake branch of the Anchorage Public Library, where a librarian would entrance a circle of moon-booted children with local Indian stories about Raven stealing the moon.

Although I'd seen plenty of coyotes, ravens had always eluded me. I'd squinted at crows in downtown alleys, on coastal beaches, clattering around trash cans, looking for the fat beak, furry throat, and muscled wing that set the legendary bird apart from its scrawny cousin. Nothing.

Until that morning. Unzipping the tent flap, I pulled on my boots and crouched in a stew of hemlock cones, needles, moss, and mud. The bird had none of the crow's glossy flash. Its blackness sucked light from the air, creating a vortex of night centered in an eye that fell gleamless into the void.

When Edgar Allan Poe was casting the lead in the poem that would become "The Raven," he looked for an animal that would set a tone of death, longing, and melancholy. He drew upon a European tradition that saw the raven as a symbol of darkness, an intermediary between the temporal and spiritual realms. The bird had earned its reputation by ruining crops and pecking at the bodies of the battlefield dead.

But Poe's ominous raven never flew into the imagination of the Pacific Northwest. Here the bird has always been a creative force at play in the land. Squatting on the bog before sunrise, I had to choose my totem: harbinger of doom or creator of magic and myth. Pack it in or push on.

One of the most enduring tales among Puget Sound tribes is the story of Raven bringing light to the world. It begins with Raven stubbing his toe. Fed up with all the stumbling in the dark, he conceives a plan to steal light from an old man who keeps the dawn in a cedar chest. One day Raven sees the old man's daughter scoop water from the river. Acting quickly, he transforms himself into a hemlock needle floating on the stream. The daughter catches the needle in her bucket and drinks. Inside her, Raven becomes a fetus and emerges some months later as a newborn son. As the son grows, he discovers the old man's secret cedar box. The son asks to see inside, but the grandfather refuses. The son asks again, and again is denied. The boy puts up such a fuss that eventually the old man opens the box. Inside is another box, and inside that another. Over time the boy pleads, whines, and badgers his grandfather into opening one box after another, smaller and smaller. Catherine Feher-Elston concludes the story in her book *Ravensong*:

"Finally, Raven had been given all of the boxes except the smallest one containing the light. A glow emanated from this box, and Raven-boy demanded it, too, as a gift from his grandfather.

"'Absolutely not,' Grandfather said. Raven-boy started crying. He howled and yowled.

"'Give it to me, give it to me. I want the box. I want to see inside,' he squawked.

"Finally, the old man relented. He opened the box and tossed it to Raven-boy. In an instant, Raven transformed into his old self, swooped down upon the light, and taking it in his beak, flew up the smokehole and out into the open sky. Raven the Transformer lit up the world."

In the deep forests of Mount Rainier, the sun doesn't rise, it leaks in thin bands through the trees. As I watched the raven that morning, brilliant shafts pierced the woodsy gloom. They struck a hemlock trunk, turned a black branch brilliant green, electrified a patch of chartreuse moss. My attention drawn by the sun, I turned back to find the raven gone. An icy drop surprised my neck and ran south. I rose, wiped it away, and began packing.

With my soggy homestead slumped on my back, I began walking. One step, two, three. Further into the mountain. Where storms and rain, fear and magic await. Where Raven brings the sun.

PRESSING
THROUGH CLOUD

When *I told friends I intended to walk* around the mountain, they worried. "You sure you're gonna be all right?" they said. "Do you have any idea what you're doing?" they meant.

The night before my departure a friend told me the story of a hiking companion stung by bees. "Got him right on the neck," she said. "He felt fine for the first half-hour—hurt like a bitch—but then his neck started swelling up so much it was tough to breathe. The Medevac guys said if they hadn't reached him when they did, he probably wouldn't have made it." I resolved to give the bees a wide berth.

My parents suggested I take a pager, a cellular phone, a walkie-talkie, a radio, a homing beacon. I considered a phone but rejected it as un-Thoreauvian. At the trailhead, where I couldn't refuse, my father pressed a vintage signal flare into my hand. I stashed it in a pocket and took comfort in knowing that if I went down I could light the torch and take an entire national park down with me.

What could go wrong?

Sprained ankle, strained back, broken leg, dislocated knee. Fall into a river. Fall into a glacier. Fall off a cliff. Bear eat your food. Bear eat you. Foot blisters. Shin splints. Food poisoning. Berry poisoning. Hypothermia. Hantavirus. Tick-borne fever. Bee sting. Flu. Lose map, lose way, lose life.

It could rain.

It rained for days everlasting, unending, without cease. Fog socked in the Tahoma Creek valley, moving among the treetops with the creeping opacity of breath on a winter's morning. Near the top of Emerald Ridge I paused and leaned on my walking stick. This is what we come to see, up high in the world: the respiration of forests.

Walking around Mount Rainier is like hiking a circle of gigantic Ws. It's all up one ridge and down the next, losing and gaining the elevation of two World Trade Centers in a day. Bette Filley wasn't kidding. When the sun shines, the Wonderland Trail is an exhausting but not unrewarding trek. When it rains, the Wonderland's a downright bitch.

One day out, I found the mist keeping my pace, over one ridge and then another. This wasn't the ground fog that sent Buicks pitching into ditches along the roads of my native Snohomish Valley. A mile above Puget Sound I pressed through cloud.

On a high ridge I slumped off my pack and ate a handful of trail mix. I added a cut of pumice to a cairn and rested against a nearby boulder. Mountains are well known as environments of extremes—extreme altitude, weather, coldness, discomfort—but nothing had prepared me for Rainier's moments of radical silence and senselessness. It was so *quiet*. Sitting in the dewy grass inside a womb of cloud, I felt at once lost and perfectly secure. My senses strained to engage the world. The cottony puff swallowed the earth and sky and my own voice as well. No wind. No birds. No mosquitoes whining for blood. The air held the fragrance of water. My eyes, searching for a focal point, found only the dim dish of the sun. I gazed at it as directly as at the moon. Everything was wet; nothing dripped.

I followed the trail through the wet grass of the meadow. A scattering of scrubby firs acted as guideposts barely visible in the ambient gauze. Their presence indicated firm ground; their absence meant I'd run out of earth. Near a high mountain pond the meadow fell away, cut clean as a cliff. I narrowed my eyes and looked harder into the illusion. The water so mirrored the haze that they were indistinguishable. The lake had become cloud.

The world's religions share a belief in mountains as places of spiritual significance. Buddhists hold a number of mountains sacred; they are the abodes of deities and spirits. The Mongols buried their leaders in high places, the better to let the dead draw upon the power of mountain spirits. In Hindu belief, Mount Meru sits at the center of the world between heaven and earth. The popular mythology of twentieth-century America continues the tradition. Who lives atop mountains? The Wicked Witch of the West and the Grinch Who Stole

Christmas. Passing through this place of spirits, I began to understand how those legends were born.

Mountains aren't just convenient symbols, the nearest point to heaven from earth. On days like this they are truly spooky and epiphanic. The clouds like ghosts slip between hemlock trunks dripping with beards of lichen. When the trees dissolve into alpine meadows and the path climbs into higher clouds, it's easy to imagine yourself approaching the gates of heaven. It would take but a moment to leap into the whiteness and become one of the people who come to Rainier and vanish. For a moment you think you understand why they do it. Walk off: It would be so easy. The absence of others makes the idea oddly comforting. There would be no screaming and weeping, no rescuers' lives put at risk. Just one's own life held in the balance. A friend once told me that the availability of death consoled her when life's terrors seemed overwhelming. On Rainier's high ridges I came close to understanding her.

The people native to Mount Rainier are uneasy about the supernatural aura of high places. To them the top of Mount Rainier is a place of powerful spirits. The son of the Yakama chief Kamiakin once described how the world began. In the beginning all the world was water and the Great Spirit lived in the sky. When it came time to make the land, the Great Spirit scooped up handfuls of mud from the shallows. He deepened the oceans and raised the soil and piled some mud so high that it froze hard and became mountains.

It's sometimes said that the Indians who live near it worship Mount Rainier as a god. This isn't true. The Nisqually Indians, who established villages along the Nisqually River from Puget Sound to the mountain until the government forced them onto reservation land in 1857, believe every manifestation of the natural world is imbued with a spirit. The mountain is no more or less a god than the river, the cedar, the salmon, the thunder, or the coyote. These spirits watch over the bodies of the visible world. In the tradition of the Nisqually and the Yakama, who live on the plains east of the mountain, when a young man came of age he was sent alone into the wilderness on a quest to discover his *tahmahnawis*, the spirit power that would guide and protect him throughout his life.

Spirits inhabited all aspects of the Nisqually world. *Doquebulth* was the spirit of good forces, *Seatco* the spirit of darkness and evil. Most spirits were a little bit *Doquebulth*, a little bit *Seatco*. *Wha-quoddie*, the storm spirit, blew ferocious weather in from the coast, but also brought the rain that nourished the camas fields and fed the salmon-filled rivers. At the center of it all was *Sagale Tyee*, the great creator, the closest Nisqually equivalent to Yahweh, God, or Allah. If there was a point at which *Sagale Tyee* rested on the earth, the Nisqually believed the summit of Mount Rainier was the most likely spot.

Powerful forces—storm, wind, volcano—ruled the world of permanent snow and stood guard over the sacred summit. In 1870, when two white men asked a Nisqually named Sluiskin to guide them to the top of Mount Rainier, he considered the idea absurd, but agreed to take them partway up. They made it as far as the snowline, where Sluiskin halted and refused to lead them any farther toward destruction. If avalanches, rockfalls, or high mountain tempests didn't kill them, the summit spirits surely would. "Finding that his words did not produce the desired effect," wrote Hazard Stevens, who made the first recorded ascent with partner Philemon Beecher Van Trump, "he assured us that, if we persisted in attempting the ascent, he would wait three days for our return, and would then proceed to Olympia and inform our friends of our death; and he begged us to give him a paper (a written note) to take to them, so that they might believe his story." Stevens and Van Trump continued to the summit and returned to tell the tale. To this day many Nisqually refuse to cross the snowline that separates the sacred from the profane.

It seems unlikely that no Indian had reached the top prior to the white men's ascent; Sluiskin's warnings to Stevens and Van Trump about the rockfalls, bitter cold, and winds strong enough to "sweep you off into space like a withered leaf" bear the accuracy of experience, not imagination. His own grandfather had climbed close to the summit once and barely escaped with his life; Sluiskin couldn't have been eager to risk his own for the sake of two climbing-mad Bostons (as white Americans were called by local Indians).

Nisqually and Yakama myths often begin with the phrase "Back when mountains were people . . . " Back when mountains were people they quarreled like wet hens. The Cascade volcanoes were often jealous wives, stealing each other's goats and berries and boxing like leviathans. Mount Hood and Mount St. Helens threw fire at each other across the Columbia River. In the stories, Mount Rainier often assumed the role of a fat angry wife. Duwamish myth depicts her as a huge woman who lived in the Olympic Mountains and squabbled incessantly with her husband's other wives. One day her husband could take no more. He picked her up and set her across Puget Sound, where there was room for her ample flanks and peace from her bickering tongue.

The Lummi, who live near the Canadian border, cast Rainier as the jealous wife of Mount Baker. Rainier was the favorite of Baker's two wives, but she had an awful temper. After a while the younger wife, Mount Shuksan, with her kind disposition, became the shine of Baker's eye. Furious, Rainier threatened to leave unless Baker showed her more attention. When Baker ignored her, she made good her threat and traveled south, alone and slow. After a distance she looked back, expecting Baker to call her home. He did not. A little farther, she looked again. Still nothing. With a heavy heart she continued on and camped for the night on the highest hill in the land. She stretched and stretched to see Baker and her children, until she stood higher than all the mountains around. But still Baker did not call her home. "Often on a clear day or a clear night," says the narrator, "the mountain dresses in sparkling white and looks with longing at Baker and the mountain children near him."

COMPANY

The rain, the rain, the rain. If it didn't strike directly, it found me in more insidious ways. In the high meadows of Indian Henry's Hunting Ground, ankle-deep lupine washed my feet. The green leather of der Wanderschuhe soaked up water with such enthusiasm that the boots earned themselves a new name: "der Waterschuhe." Two days into my trek, the sweet mountain of my affection was turning nasty and cold.

Indian Henry's was named for a Klickitat Indian who settled on a farm near Eatonville in the 1880s and guided some of the first climbers through his hunting ground for two dollars a day. A prosperous farmer with three wives, Henry was known for his well-developed sense of property rights. Philemon Van Trump once saw a sign on Henry's barn door that read: "Notice: Any one entering here is liable to instant death, as I have set spring guns inside. To all whom it may concern. Indian Henry."

"It probably was only a bluff," wrote historian Aubrey Haines, "for he was really a kind man."

Descending in the early afternoon from Indian Henry's, I found myself shuffling through a car wash of leaves. Wet hands of fireweed, paintbrush, and devil's club slapped me as I passed. The icy splash soaked my arms and chest and gave absolute fits to The Renegade. I was as sorely wet as I have been in my life.

We sidestep weather in cities, scuttling from building to car to porch. "The approaching storm" is a hollow phrase in the city, where it's impossible to see much of anything approach, let alone witness a storm ride a five-mile sky. Skyscrapers shrink our view to a series of slots. We live in trenches. On the mountain, weather can't be ignored or outrun; it is the dominant fact of life and can sometimes seem the manifestation of a cruel god.

The rain is here because of the mountain. Warm, moist air from the Pacific Ocean flows over Western Washington and bumps into the Cascade Range. The air cools and condenses into clouds; it rains. From on high it looks as if a barn of cotton blew in and snagged on the jagged ridges of the Cascades. Given the right conditions, the mountain can whip up its own self-contained storm. Rainier's glacial ice often cools atmospheric moisture into a lenticular cloud that hovers over the peak like a dinner plate; summit storms with one-hundred-mile-an-hour winds can rage within a cloudcap on an otherwise clear day.

The Pacific Northwest boasts a long and honorable tradition of rain-soaked misery. One of its earliest and perhaps best descriptions was recorded nearly two centuries ago by the great American explorer and abysmal speller William Clark. Clark spent a winter on the Oregon-Washington coast, which is to rain what the Antarctic is to snow. "Rained all the after part of last night, rain continues this morning," he wrote in late 1805. "We are all wet cold and disagreeable." During their coastal wintering, Lewis and Clark and their Corps of Discovery enjoyed a total of twelve days without rain. At one point it poured for eleven days straight "without a longer intermition than 2 hours at a time."

In his journal Clark repeats the word *disagreeable* as if it were a mantra. It's a curiously evocative description. *Miserable* would be the natural choice, but Clark's adjective captures a quality of the Northwestern damp that, as Ken Kesey once wrote, you have to go through a winter to understand. The stuff puts you on edge. It feels as if nobody's showered or shaved in three days. The civility that Northwesterners wear like hand lotion washes away; some snap at one another, some just snap. About the ninth or tenth day, everybody looks at each other and says, "God*damn* it's been raining." That is what William Clark felt, I think. On November 15, 1805, he wrote: "The rainney weather continued . . . from the 5th in the morng. untill the 16th is eleven days rain, and the most disagreeable time I have experienced . . . " Cold, wet, cooped up, and hungry, I imagine Clark waking to the sound of skyspatter on the morning of the 16th and thinking: I can't *believe* this shit.

I imagine it because that is what I thought when I awoke on the mountain. To more rain.

Day three, still wet. During the night I dreamed I was an ultramarathon runner who had set out to break the speed record for circumnavigation of the mountain, which is something like twenty-nine hours. Everything went fine for the first few hours, but then obstacles began cropping up. First it was normal stuff like downed trees, but after a while the trail led into a bizarro land where rivers flowed above me and the trail melted like Dalí's clock down cliffs. I took it in stride. At one point I passed my pack-heavy self chuffing along the trail and thought, *What a Barney.* I woke at dawn, disconsolate at finding myself trapped in the pathetic musculature of the Barney.

Two hours later, having traded a warm sleeping bag for a clammy shirt and spongy socks, I began walking and found that my legs, toughened by two days of ridge climbing, turned like pistons. At the top of the first ridge, I broke for lunch and decided to press on to Golden Lakes, eight miles north and two thousand feet of ridge above me. Nothing but melted trail could stop me.

Two hours later my body broke down. It's a downhill skip from Klapatche Ridge to the Puyallup River, then a long slog up to Golden Lakes. My pace slowed. I took three stops an hour instead of two, then four. The Renegade grew unruly. Each time the pack came off I risked shoulder dislocations and muscle tears in returning it to its six-four perch, and each time it seemed to gain weight from contact with the ground. Like der Waterschuhe, The Renegade earned its *nom de guerre*: The Wrencher. My mind was tempted by the thought of caving in here. Right on the trail. Throw off The Wrencher, shuck der Waterschuhe. Pitch the tent, to hell with the other hikers. They wouldn't be along anyway. In September the trails were so deserted, I was lucky to pass two hikers all day.

With my will draining away, I became my own coach.

"Come on. The ridge is just up ahead."

Trying. *Huff.* Must rest. *Huff.*

"You pussy. Grandmothers do this trail."

Grandmothers. *Huff.* Better shape than . . . *Huff* . . . me.

"Keep moving, Barcott!"

Bipedal motion has never come easy to me. I've always been slow. At eight years I was the slowest boy on the soccer team, and at eighteen I was the slowest athlete in any sport, including chess. My baseball teammates once named me "Piano" because when I rounded third base, I ran as if I carried one. One particular exercise tormented my youth—on soccer fields, hockey rinks, basketball courts, and baseball diamonds. The team lines up on the near end line and sprints to the near free throw line, then back to the end line, then to the half court line, back to the end line, to the far free throw line, and so on in a reversal of Zeno's arrow. Coaches traveled to the far reaches of their vocabularies to find idiosyncratic names for this torment: Liners, Crushers, Killers. With each completed section the gap between the swift and the slow widened, until the moment when the rest of the boys finished their final lap a full court-length ahead, leaving me to complete my assignment on a court empty except for the shreds of dignity trailing behind me.

One mile later the coach had lost his effectiveness. He could word-whip me all he wanted. He could kick me off the team. I didn't care. I turned to my physical therapist.

"We're walking here. That's all we're doing."

Right. *Huff.* Walking.

"That's it. Step. One, two. Right, left."

Left. *Huff.* Right. *Huff.* Left. Rest. Left. Rest.

"No no no! Step with me now. Forward."

The spoken words goaded me and gave me something to wrap my mind around. I sang songs. "I am the raaaiiin king!" By late afternoon my mind had dulled so much that I sang "Rocky Raccoon" continuously. Mile after mile I filled the forest with the tale of Rocky's met match and in my lucid moments made up prologues and epilogues. Rocky's refrain became such torture that once I shouted, "Oh for the love of Christ! Not Gideon's fucking Bible again!"

These are the early warning signs for hypothermia: exhaustion, shivering, stumbling, mild confusion. Late that afternoon, near the top of Sunset Park, I found myself batting four for four. My mind was aware enough to know it was slipping into nature's cold narcosis. The trail weaved when I walked, but straightened each time I stopped. My fingers glowed with piggish translucence.

I collapsed next to a hemlock stump. Eyes closed, I lay in the rapture of darkness.

Survival alarms rang in my head. Sleep was not the optimal response to a cooling body. I needed warmth, dryness, and fuel. Everything I owned was soaked, the tinder around Sunset Park had been marinating in clouds for the past three days, but I did have food. I tore open a blueberry breakfast bar and forced myself to chew. Gagging as the first bar went down, I found a second and a third and ate them, too. As I sat chewing granola and fruit paste, I ran my trembling hands through the soil. It was the color of toast crumbs, which made me think of a beach on Kauai where the grains were similarly golden and the water was warm and if you lay back and closed your eyes you could almost—

Get up or you'll die here, I told myself. I rose and I walked and I sang, only now the songs weren't even bad pop tunes. I'd regressed into the corner of the mind where jingles are stored.

"*Flint*-stones, meet the Flintstones, they're a modern stone age fam-uh-lee," I sang, loudly.

"Oh those Golden Grahams, crispy Golden Grahams, chunks of honey, just a touch, and grahams of golden wheat." I argued with myself: *Chunks* of honey doesn't make sense. Hmm-hm-hm-hm, just a touch. Ah—*golden* honey, just a touch, *on* grahams of golden wheat. Yes.

"*Flint*-stones, meet the Flintstones . . . "

Most people expect their waning thoughts to be of family, friends, and loved ones. My head filled with lowbrow pleasures, petty joys that have brought me happiness. The soundtrack to *Jesus Christ Superstar*. Sipping champagne in a warm bath on a cold winter's night. Eating Cherry Garcia ice cream in front of an air conditioner on an August afternoon in New York City. Christmas lights.

I rounded a corner and, in mid-Flintstones flourish, nearly ran over two hikers brooding over a map.

"Need some company?" is what I imagined myself saying.

"OH THANK *GOD!* PEOPLE! I LOVE YOU!" is what came out of my mouth.

I often felt at sea in the mountain's thick cloudbanks and at times regretted that I wasn't actually *at* sea, as the sea at least afforded the cheerful camaraderie of sailors who'd call out a greeting and perhaps hove to for an hour to exchange tidings. In ordinary circumstance, the hiker's code seemed to require silence or a cursory phrase of passing acknowledgment.

"How you doing?"

"How's it going?"

Neither hiker pauses to answer the other, because it isn't a question but rather a way of saying, "I'd rather you weren't here blemishing my experience of nature but I see that you are, and to avoid seeming rude I'll feign interest in your well-being." Since for many the point of hiking is to escape the company of other people, the sight of another on the trail is only a reminder of how far short of that goal they have fallen. I was a bad hiker, not only talking to others but cluttering up the air with words spoken to myself. To me, every passing hiker was assurance that I would not die alone in a mountain cloud.

Twenty minutes after embarrassing myself with Flintstones opera, I found myself sitting on the porch of the Golden Lakes ranger's cabin with three hikers who had water dripping off the ends of their noses. More people! I rocked against the cabin and beamed. Around us mist enveloped the lakes. A few words passed about who was continuing to the north and east sides of the mountain, who was bagging out at Mowich Lake, who had seen some animals. I tend to laugh when I'm extremely happy, which gets me into trouble in situations like this. Everything the three men said struck me as riotously funny, and I gritted my teeth to keep from bursting out laughing.

"Yep. I tell you, you want to see some bear, the east side's the place to be."

I pinched myself.

"Saw some mountain goats couple days ago up Emerald Ridge."

I smothered my face with a wet glove.

"Uh-huh."

Stop it.

"Tell you, this shit keeps up I'ma turn in at Mowich."

Turning my head, I coughed. Tears welled.

The klatch disbanded before I could humiliate myself; we broke dispirited, resigned to another night of damp misery. I huddled in my sleeping bag and waited for darkness to come. I slept and dreamed of warm houses.

Civilization proceeds in a direction opposite from everything mountains represent: starvation, hardship, coldness, the constant scramble to survive. We assume we'll live to age sixty-eight or seventy-five, and keep actuarial tables to prove it. Seat belts, air bags, meat inspectors, booster shots, exit signs, out-swinging doors, smoke alarms, inflatable vests, safety glass, bicycle helmets, electrical grounds—every day we encounter a thousand systems and products created to decrease the likelihood that we will die. People used to avoid mountains, but now we seek their company. We come for the pretty sights, but also to find a place still free from those life-saving constraints. We come to the mountain seeking beauty and terror.

Rainier provides both. The day before, on Emerald Ridge, I had watched the clouds drift away for a moment to reveal the full measure of the mountain. Above me ran the iron-orange Tahoma Glacier and the bony finger of Success Cleaver. Marmots chased each other across a grassy park and broadcast unnerving cries. The scene unsettled me. I'd been unsure about climbing Rainier from the moment my father broached the subject. Certainly I was curious about the summit—who wasn't?—but something troubled me about attacking the mountain as if it were a quarterly sales goal. At that moment on Emerald Ridge, further doubt rushed in. I felt something like the awe that struck the eighteenth-century poets in the Alps. It seemed inappropriate, even affrontive, to swing an ice axe into Rainier's flanks. Talk of "conquering" this or any mountain seemed absurd. At that moment I felt like sinking to my knees in worship.

Hindu mythology holds that the sun circumambulates Mount Meru, the center of the universe, as a gesture of respect. Looking up at the mountain that day on Emerald Ridge, watching a stain of clouds ride in and draw its appearance to a close, I thought: *What if the point is* not *to climb? Why lessen its power by slinging rope up its face?* "All my life," wrote Mary Oliver, "and it has not come to any more than this: beauty and terror." I wondered if going higher would intensify Rainier's awful splendor, tip the balance of beauty and terror, or merely drain its mystery.

At Mowich Lake, four days into the journey, I quit the mountain. The inexorable moist had crept into the cells of my sleeping bag. I could have filled a bath with the water from my wrung-out socks. My boots were terminally damp. I no longer bothered to hang my wet underwear in the tent, because the cotton absorbed more dew than it shed. I shivered more than a healthy man should. Without dry gear my next encounter with hypothermia would likely be my last. I retired for the winter, beaten.

THE ONLY SENSIBLE AND
SUITABLE NAME

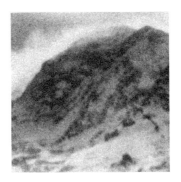

O ver winter the mountain remained cloaked behind cloud and mist, but I saw Rainier everywhere I went. Rainier Beer. Rainier Hardware. Rainier Investment. Rainier Legal Clinic. Rainier Family Dentistry. The name became one of those words whose meaning you discover and then see all over the place, as if somebody switched the signs. Rainier Nissan-Mazda. Rainier Air Systems. Rainier Case Management. Rainier House Movers. Rainier Steel. I entertained the notion of patronizing only businesses named Rainier. Rainier Catering. Rainier Charters. Rainier BBQ. Rainier Cellular Service. Rainier Helicopter Logging and Rainier Wood Recycling, the alpha and omega of forest harvestry. The word lost meaning in its repetition. Ray-neer. Rayner. Rain ear.

What did it mean? I thumbed James Phillips's reliable *Washington State Place Names*: "Vancouver named it for the grandson of Huguenot refugees whose French name was anglicized in pronunciation to 'Rainy-er' and Americanized to 'Ray-neer.' Since British Adm. Peter Rainier gained fame for defeat of American colonists in the Revolutionary War, the name has been deemed inappropriate and subjected to agitation for change." Phillips's entry struck me as a touch diplomatic, the phrasing of a writer not entirely disinterested in the "agitation." A few weeks later I had lunch with a friend who called the mountain "Tahoma." She said it with hushed reverence, as if she were afraid the mountain might hear. Tahoma was what Native Americans called it, she told me, before Europeans stamped "Rainier" on the peak. It occurred to me that there were worse ways to know a mountain than by restoring its rightful name. I had no idea I was about to step into a nomenclatorial battle that stretched back more than one hundred years.

On the morning of May 8, a Tuesday in 1792, Captain George Vancouver rounded Marrowstone Point, just south of what is now Port Townsend, and caught sight of a round, snowy mountain he'd glimpsed the previous day. He christened the peak "Mount Rainier" in honor of a colleague of recent acquaintance, Captain Peter Rainier. Vancouver's journal reveals nothing more about Rainier or the mountain; he likely was attending to more pressing matters: Earlier that morning he and his crew had sailed past two freshly severed heads on pikes.

"Mount Rainier" took hold thanks to Vancouver's charts, which were so accurate that they remained the navigational standard for the next half-century. But in the mid-nineteenth century, "Tahoma" entered the vernacular of white traders and settlers, who adopted the word from local Indians. Confusion attended the name from the start. William Fraser Tolmie, a young Glaswegian doctor who came to the Northwest in the 1830s, noted in his private journal that the Indians called the mountain "Puskehouse." A few months later, however, Tolmie hired Lachalet, a Nisqually man, and Nuckalkat, a Puyallup, to guide him to the mountain's treeline and discovered that they had a different name for it: "Tuchoma."

"Tacoma" didn't receive widespread attention until 1862 when it appeared in *The Canoe and the Saddle*, the popular travelogue of Theodore Winthrop, a Boston Brahmin who had toured the region in the 1850s. "Of all the peaks from California to Fraser's River," Winthrop wrote, "the one before me was royalest. Mount Regnier Christians have dubbed it, in stupid nomenclature, perpetuating the name of somebody or nobody. More melodiously the Siwashes call it Tacoma—a generic name also applied to all snow peaks." In 1868 Winthrop's bestseller inspired the founders of Commencement City, on the southern shore of Puget Sound, to rename their town Tacoma.

The earliest campaign to rename the mountain began, like so much in the Pacific Northwest, as a railroad marketing scheme. In the March 1883 edition of *Northwest Magazine*, a tout sheet published by the Northern Pacific Railroad to attract immigrants, the editor announced that the mountain standing over the railroad's western terminus would henceforth be called Mount Tacoma in its guidebooks and publications. The change was ordered by Charles Wright, a Philadelphia land baron and Northern Pacific director who had steered the terminus to Tacoma and who, as president of the Tacoma Land Company, had no small interest in publicizing the city's name. For a while it worked. In 1886 a correspondent for the *Overland Monthly* reported that "the name of Rainier is being gradually supplanted by the Indian appellation of Tacoma (pronounced Tachoma, with the German guttural sound to the ach), a name not only more appropriate on account of its antiquity, but to be preferred on account of its euphony."

Tacoma's early prosperity emboldened the advocates of "Mount Tacoma." Completion of the Northern Pacific railhead in 1883 brought boomtime to the city. Westward immigrants turned the village of 1,098 people in 1880 into a city of 36,006 by 1890—a city that challenged the dominance of the 42,000-strong Seattle. Confidence ran so high that some Tacoma boosters suggested that Washington state change its name to The State of Tacoma.

Then Tacoma's good fortune faltered. In 1892 the newly formed U.S. Board on Geographic Names issued its inaugural report, a list of about two thousand official American place names. To counteract the thousands of free "Mount Tacoma" maps distributed by the Northern Pacific, the board ruled that Washington state's high peak be named "Rainier, Mt." Tacomans suspected foul play. An apocryphal story circulated about the Seattle Brewing and Malting Company delivering free kegs of Rainier Beer to a late-night geographic board meeting. The story gained credence only in Tacoma, where the town fathers gathered for a fight.

The Tacoma Commercial Club hired British Arctic adventurer Frederick Schwatka to explore the mountain, scout new trails, and write a book celebrating "Mount Tacoma." Unfortunately for Tacoma,

Lieutenant Schwatka's explorations went astray. In his off-hours the lieutenant enjoyed roaming the Pacific Northwest's seamier districts, which in the 1890s were legendary. (The very term "skid row" comes from Seattle's skid road, a logging skid at the center of a large liquor and prostitution industry.) At three a.m. on November 2, 1892, six weeks after Schwatka's Tacoma debut, a policeman in Portland, Oregon, rolled a passed-out drunk from a First Street gutter. Lieutenant Frederick Schwatka lay in disgrace, a bottle of laudanum tinkling at his hip. Two hours later he was dead.

The city pressed on without him. Early the next year Mount Tacoma advocates gathered at the Tacoma Academy of Science to hear Judge James Wickersham argue their cause. Wickersham blasted "Rainier," with written testimonials from Indians, soldiers, famous writers, and pioneer climbers. All testified to the rightful claim of "Tacoma," but everyone had a different interpretation of the word: "the mountain," "the snow mountain," "rumbling noise," "nourishing breast," "near to heaven," "the gods," "friend at first sight," and "the place from which you get coal." This confusion went unnoted in Wickersham's brief; Mount Tacoma advocates would regret the oversight.

The federal government stepped up its protection of the mountain due in part to the publicity generated by Tacoma's campaign. In 1893 the U.S. Department of the Interior preserved a twenty-thousand-acre skirt around the peak and called it the Pacific Forest Reserve. Five years later Congress voted to expand the reserve and rename it "Washington National Park." Tacomans weren't thrilled with the name, though they were pleased to see their mountain protected. But before President William McKinley could sign the act creating the park, an Iowa congressman named John Lacy slipped in a midnight amendment replacing

"Washington" with the name of the grandson of Huguenot refugees: On March 2, 1899, President McKinley signed "Mount Rainier National Park" into existence.

At first Tacoma's campaign to rename Rainier struck me as folly, Tacomans' delusion of grandeur. But as I spent more time on the mountain I came to sympathize with Judge Wickersham. Despite the West's reputation for rugged individualism, much of the real power in the territory's early days was exercised by Eastern and Midwestern bankers, railroad tycoons, and lumber concerns. Sometimes all the early settlers owned was the land they lived on. Their sense of ownership strengthened after they had survived a winter or two, living through hard times and hard weather. Changing the name to Mount Tacoma would have been a bold act of cultural reclamation, a proclamation that the mountain belonged to the people who lived with it, not to the British Admiralty and the geographic names board. (The irony of whites restoring the mountain's Native name while stealing the Nisqually and Yakama land around it couldn't have been lost on Northwest Indians.)

That the same impulse to ownership exists today testifies to the cultural power of the mountain. When visitors drop in and stake an unearned claim, we look at them as poachers. The impulse may be ungenerous—*This is ours, not yours*—but it can't be denied. I've felt it myself. A few years ago I took a grand-opening tour of a shopping mall—the SuperMall of the Great Northwest in Auburn. The mall's construction manager, who hailed from back East, told us how she'd developed a great love for Mount Rainier. Whenever it came into view, she said, she'd call friends and tell them, "Look! My mountain's out!" Steam escaped from my ears.

By early 1917 public opinion had swung Tacoma's way. "The fact is that nobody likes the name 'Mount Rainier,'" said U.S. Interior Secretary Franklin Lane. Newspapers around the nation adopted "Mount Tacoma" as their house style. Even Helen Keller, in town on a lecture tour, agreed that "Mount Tacoma" seemed "the only sensible and suitable name." Sam Wall, a Tacoma newspaperman who once shot a man for questioning his hometown loyalty, adopted the name change as his personal crusade. Wall's perseverance earned him a hearing before the U.S. Board on Geographic Names, but his testimony failed to sway the board. "No geographic feature in any part of the world can claim a name more firmly fixed" than Mount Rainier, declared chairman C. Hart Merriam in his May 1917 ruling. Wall's cause came undone partly because nobody could prove which version of "Tacoma" was correct, or what the word even meant. In the years since Judge Wickersham's call to arms, the etymology of "Tacoma" had grown ever more confused. Because Pacific Northwest Indian languages are exclusively oral, any of a dozen phonetic renderings might be accurate. Among those offered were Tacoma, Tahoma, Tahoba, Takhoma, Tachoma, Tachkoma, Tagoma, Taghoma, Tachhoma, Tachkoma, Tacobah, Takoman, Takeman, Ry-ah-ku, Ta-ho-bet, Ta-ko-bet, Tacobet, Tacobed, Tacob, Tacoba, Tacope, Dacobed, Tahchobet, Tahobet, T'koma, T'choba, T'chakoba, Tach-ho-ma, Tahhohmah, Tahkobed, Takeman, Takob, Takobid, Takoman, Takkobud, Haik-Tacomas, Puskehouse, Tuahku, Tawauk, Twauk, Tuhkobud, Twahwauk, Stiquak, Yalemite, Nebat, Tiswauk, and Sawhle Tyiee. One expert claimed "Tacoma" originated with the Algonquin Indians and traveled across the continent on the tongues of various tribes; another believed the word originated in Mongolia. Others argued that the word came out of Japan, or was invented by Spanish or Norwegian explorers. C. Hart Merriam had little patience for Tacoma's flimsy case. The Puyallup and Nisqually tribes near the mountain called it "Tuahku," "Stiquak," and "Puskehouse." "Has any citizen of Tacoma," wrote Merriam, "ever suggested the adoption of any one of them?"

Tacoma fretted about its mountain while entire industries skipped town. In 1920 the Northern Pacific Railroad, Tacoma's raison d'être, moved its operations north to Seattle. "As children we didn't care about the loss of the termini," recalled historian and native Tacoman Murray Morgan. "What bothered us was the loss of our Mountain."

No straw was too brittle to be grasped. In 1921 a group of Civil War veterans petitioned the geographic names board to change Mount Rainier's name to "Mount Lincoln." Before dismissing the claim, the board heard Colonel Beverly Coiner of Tacoma entreat the government to nullify "Rainier" because of a typo. In Vancouver's *Voyage of Discovery to the North Pacific Ocean and Round the World*, Coiner testified, the British navigator sites the peak at "N. 42 E." from Marrowstone Point, a spot halfway between Mount Baker and Glacier Peak, about one hundred miles north of Mount Rainier.

It was just a typo. Mount Rainier's position should have read "S. 42 E." But the colonel's contention enticed me. I bought a plastic protractor at a neighborhood drugstore and traced directional rays across a Rand McNally road atlas. The colonel had a point! By centering the protractor at Marrowstone Point and marking off 42 degrees, my pencil cruised across Puget Sound, mowed through Issaquah, and ended up burrowed in a flattish section of southeastern King County. Impossible. I checked again. The adrenaline of a scoop rushed within my reporter's brain. I spent an excited hour imagining myself announcing George Vancouver's two-hundred-year-old deception. This must have been how Colonel Coiner felt. Why had no one listened to him?

Before I bumbled further down the colonel's path, a friend whose knowledge of compasses wasn't limited to N, S, E, and W broke the news that Vancouver knew something about magnetic variation that the colonel and I did not. The Earth's longitudinal lines converge at the true North Pole, but the globe's shifting magnetic fields meet farther south, in Canada's Queen Elizabeth Islands. The difference between geographic north and magnetic north is a given area's variation. Protractor in hand, I adjusted the setting for Puget Sound's variation of 22 degrees, at which point Mount Rainier intersected the plastic dimple exactly 42 degrees east from south. Having felt Beverly Coiner's excitement, I was able to empathize with the humiliation that must have begun the moment I imagine a member of the geographic names board said, *Pardon me, Colonel, but if you'll adjust your reading by 22 degrees . . .*

Even so, one wonders how Coiner imagined Vancouver spotting, where's that atlas . . . *Gee Mountain* (5,030 feet) and missing the 14,000-foot colossus dominating the entire Puget Sound. In the colonel's world, and for an hour mine as well, Vancouver stood a mad wizard on the bridge, indulging no *But sir's* from his men and bellowing, *Pay no attention to that mountain in the east!*

In January 1924, at the request of Mount Tacoma advocates, the Washington, D.C., chapter of the Sons of the American Revolution publicly endorsed "Mount Tacoma," signaling the beginning of the final bitter fight against "Rainier," one that would be fought with the weapons of the desperate: character assassination and patriotic gore. With the SAR's backing, Senator C. C. Dill of Washington state, introduced federal legislation to change the name to Mount Tacoma.

As the campaign progressed, Peter Rainier became a target of outrage and ridicule. Mount Rainier advocates recast his gallant action in the American Revolutionary War as pernicious treason. The *San Francisco Journal* ridiculed him as "King George III's fat old Admiral." A Manchester, New Hampshire, editorial described him as a pirate, a murderer of women, and "a fiend in human form." An editorial cartoonist depicted "that old blighter Rainier" as a white-wigged fool hoisting a pint of Rainier Beer; another supplied him with a crag tooth and a witch's nose.

In fact, Peter Rainier was no pirate, no murderer, and nobody's fool. He did, however, *look* peculiar—at least in the portrait of him that's come down to us: His white hair marks him as a man well past his sailing days—he was sixty-four at the sitting—and the portraitist has done embarrassingly well in capturing the rumpled bulge of belly that has sprung Rainier's southernmost vest button from its embroidered constraints. The man in the picture gazes calmly past our right shoulder, years on land having stripped this admiral of the whip-cracking glare evident in so many portraits of his colleagues. He does not exude the confidence of Caesar. What stands out above all are his glasses: spectacles like bicycle tires. Naked before God and his mountain, the admiral could barely see.

He did other things well, chiefly winning naval battles and accumulating the spoils of empire. Rainier went to sea at fifteen and saw action in the East Indies before leaving the service eight years later. At twenty-six he rejoined the Navy as a lieutenant and worked his way up under the command of Sir Alan Gardner, under whom Vancouver also served. Rainier served in the West Indies before being awarded his own ship, the *Ostrich,* in time to enter the American Revolutionary War. In July 1778 the *Ostrich* traded cannon fire with the *Polly*, an American privateer near Savannah, Georgia. Rainier's breast caught a ball from a *Polly* musket, but he refused to relinquish command, staying on to direct the fight against the better-armed American brig. The *Polly* surrendered after three hours, having seen her captain and more than two dozen men die in the battle. The *Ostrich* lost seven men.

After his brush with mortality, Rainier sailed to the East Indies before returning home in 1790 to serve in the Channel Fleet, England's main line of defense against France. There he met and befriended George Vancouver. Within the year both men set sail for opposite ends of the globe. Rainier returned east while Vancouver went west to survey Alaska and the American Northwest. In financial terms, Rainier's was the wiser choice. The trouble with uncharted land is that it's very often empty. In the 1790s Alaska and the Pacific Northwest were bare cupboards, bootywise. The years when British crews could trade a handful of trinkets for a treasure of sea otter pelts were long past. Fur traders in the 1790s dealt with Indians who knew the meaning of market price.

The East Indies, key ports in the spice trade, were veritable warehouses of wealth. British naval officers playing by eighteenth-century rules stood to win a fortune in battle prizes. When a ship's captain took a town, he *took* the *town.* In February 1796, Rainier led five heavily armed ships into the port of Amboyna, in what are now the Moluccan islands of Indonesia, and scooped up both the town and a Dutch brig without firing a shot. Two weeks later he stormed into nearby Banda Neira and accepted the surrender of the Banda Islands by sunset. At both places Rear Admiral Rainier, following common practice, commandeered stores of valuable spices before strolling into the local treasury and withdrawing sackfuls of the public trust. A captain's share of the Amboyna and Banda Neira prize money is said to have been 15,000 pounds sterling. Bear in mind, the yearly wage for a rear admiral was 637 pounds; medium-rank officers (lieutenants and such) went to sea for a mere 8 pounds per month. In Patrick O'Brian's novel *H.M.S. Surprise*, a grizzled seaman making passage to the East Indies advises a young sailor hoping to find fortune in the spice islands that "not since Admiral Rainier cleaned up Trincomalee" had there been much in the way of spoils for an honest seaman to claim.

Unlike his contemporary William Bligh, Peter Rainier was no keel-hauling killjoy. Upon his retirement in 1805, Rainier's men gave him a rousing sendoff at a Madras banquet hall fitted with fine linen and chandeliers. Caskets of claret fueled dozens of toasts and drunken songs composed for the occasion:

And tho' relentless Time hath spread
His silver honours o'er his head,
While Commerce *triumphs in India's fame,*
Rainier! *her happy sons shall venerate thy name.*

The rear admiral did not retire from table until three o'clock in the morning.

Despite the acclaim in Madras and a 250,000-pound fortune back home, Peter Rainier disappeared from English memory with sobering haste. The *Naval Chronicle*, the journal of record for His Majesty's fleet, recorded the deaths of ten notable officers in its 1808 edition. Some were killed in gallant attack; others died of mundane afflictions ("a mortification in his foot"). The final entry contained a single line: "Lately, at Bath, Admiral Rainier."

The U.S. Senate voted to rename the peak Mount Tacoma in April 1924, but the bill stalled in the House of Representatives. The House Committee on Public Lands, preoccupied with the Teapot Dome scandal, held a one-day hearing on the matter before referring it to a council more experienced in the ways of place names: the Board on Geographic Names.

The names board was tired of Tacoma's game, and took pains to refute the city's case, going so far as to mock Tacoma's Anglophobia: "If our sense of patriotism should lead us to cancel English names because we were once at war with England, would not the map of the United States look like a skinned cat?" With the names board against it, Tacoma's cause fell apart. During the House hearings, the *Tacoma News Tribune* railed against Seattle's attempt to "pack the room with their clackers," but Seattle needn't have bothered. The tide had turned. The bill failed by a vote of nine to four.

In the decades since, the Mount Tacoma cause has mouldered in Washington state's cabinet of odd causes. In 1939 the Tacoma Chamber of Commerce agreed to use "Mount Rainier" in its promotional literature, ending the city's official role in the campaign. At the office of the state Board on Geographic Names, in Olympia, the file on Mount Rainier contains only two recent challenges. One includes a recording of Spokane native Bing Crosby scolding the people of Puget Sound for abandoning Mount Tacoma. The other was filed in 1984 by a New Age guru who believed the mountain housed an ancient race of space aliens that had built a landing strip near Ashford to facilitate their homecoming. Both claims were dismissed.

AERIAL PLANKTON

ver winter the mountain reclaims its territory. From Seattle its shoulders rise and extend and it looks as if the entire chain of Cascadian mountains has flowed out of Rainier's caldera. So much snow falls on Mount Rainier that you can walk up to the Paradise Inn and look into its third-story windows without a ladder. The same weather pattern that douses the lower mountain with rain dumps about 600 inches of snow on Paradise every winter. Some winters it snows so much you think the sun's never coming back. During the winter of 1971–72 more than 93 feet (1,122 inches, exactly) of snow buried Paradise. Each year from November through April, the entire park shuts down except for the Longmire-to-Paradise road, which crews keep open by plowing continually.

On the lower reaches of the mountain, winter rain and snow eats away at civilization's relentless paving project. In the late 1980s a series of glacial floods wiped out a section of West Side Road, a tourist drive that dead-ended halfway to Mowich Lake. The floods turned an already primitive road into Fish Creek. Two months after my aborted Wonderland trek, November's rainy floods poured out of the mountain and continued the reclamation project.

During a lull in the storms, I bicycled up the remains of West Side Road and saw how quickly all trace of human incursion could vanish. Deep veins cut through the path. I braided through mounds of mud, rocks, and limbs. The mountain, which hadn't been "out" for weeks, remained locked in heavy vapor. Glacial flour milking up Tahoma Creek offered the only clue that the big icegrind was still in business up high. I stopped to listen to the creek turn its boulders and devour its banks, remaking its bed minute by minute. I rode past drooping cedars and lightning-struck hemlocks and a secret glade where emerald moss comforts the forest floor. Three miles up the road, knee-deep mud forced me to abandon my bike. On the south side of Dry Creek, I looked down to see my feetless legs disappear into the gooey muck. I pulled one out with a *slurp* and set it on a boulder, which sank as the other foot emerged from the liquid road. Across the creek I boulder-hopped, the rocks burbling into quickmud as fast as I could bound. At a spot where I remembered a concrete stream culvert having been, I dug through the mudwash with a cedar branch. Through a yard of mountain I dug and still couldn't reach the old bunker. The next summer it took a bulldozer crew five days to uncover it.

When the cold season made solo travel too dangerous, I went snowshoeing with Skip Card, an old college friend who had been hiking Rainier since he was old enough to walk. Skip's family owned a vacation trailer on an alder-shaded swamp near the mountain. The trailer was so small that I once stood in the living room and set my shirt on fire with the kitchen stove. Since Skip's shift at a local newspaper ended around midnight, we'd meet at the trailer at two in the morning and he'd tell me what was on tomorrow's front page before we drifted off to sleep. He made excellent trail conversation, kept a steady pace, and recited the poetry of Robert Service when drunk.

It was best to ski or shoe behind Skip, because I stopped to examine the trees and rivers and snow, and he did not. One day I spent an entire afternoon obsessing about the turquoise blue that glowed in the pits punched out by our ski poles. It was as if we'd cut the snow and out flowed the sky. But what most caught my attention were the bugs.

We tend to think of snow as sterile. But if you keep your eyes to the ground, you'll see nations of insects thriving in the crystal drifts. The larger bugs—the wolf spiders and jumping spiders, the rove beetles, daddy longlegs, and earwigs—stand out against the white backdrop so starkly that they fairly advertise themselves to hungry crows and jays. If you drop to hands and knees and crawl around, you'll discover millipedes, snow scorpionflies, and colonies of microscopic snow fleas so numerous and hidden that the habit of slaking a thirst with snow will be forever broken.

I met an entomologist one day in a coffeehouse in Seattle's Capitol Hill district and we talked about these winter insects. Ed Lisowski had long stringy hair and the laid-back air of a guy who went to a lot of

Foghat concerts. We talked about springtails and snow scorpionflies and he showed me some specimens he kept in a tackle box in his truck.

A few weeks later Ed and I hiked up West Side Road to Fish Creek in search of the tiniest creature on the mountain: the snow flea. A gray jay thrashed a trout fingerling to bite-size pieces on the rocks of a river-bar a few yards away from us, two grown men creeping over mud and snow in December. Every once in a while Ed bent over and sucked a suspicious-looking crawler into a vacuum hose. After examining each one he returned it to the mud. Park officials, he told me, were uptight about people taking anything out of the park.

"You finding anything?" I asked.

"Nothing exciting," Ed said.

My hands were cold. My nose ran. Just as I began to get that we're-gonna-get-skunked feeling that usually comes when I'm baiting a pole, Ed got a strike.

"Over here," he shouted. "Here's a population that's exploding."

Ed had his nose in a patch of rotten bracken, prime feeding ground for the fungus-hungry flea. I joined him and saw nothing until my forehead grazed the snow, and then I saw them everywhere, bugs no larger than a hangnail on your pinkie, crawling between grains of corn snow as easily as a child slips through a jungle gym.

A British entomologist once calculated that a billion billion insects are alive at every moment. Of the 1.82 million named plants and animals, more than one million are insects, which account for five of every six animal species. Many scientists suspect our catalogue is nowhere near complete. Estimates of a complete insect species survey range from two million to eighty million. If you imagine the diversity of life spread over a clock face, mammals account for about one tick of the minute hand. Arthropods take up more than three-quarters of an hour. Insects live in the coldest reaches of the Arctic and the hottest stretches of desert. Himalayan climbers have nearly spiked spiders on their crampons near the summit of Mount Everest. One of the most famous aphorisms in science is the British biologist J. B. S. Haldane's answer to the question, What might one conclude about God based on a study of His creation? "An inordinate fondness for beetles." In the race for species diversity, beetles overwhelm us all. The order *Coleoptera* counts more than 400,000 members. *Mammalia* taps out at around 8,000. Haldane's friend Kenneth Kermack once wrote in his defense, "Haldane was making a theological point: God is most likely to take trouble over reproducing his own image, and his 400,000 attempts at the perfect beetle contrast with his slipshod creation of man. When we meet the Almighty face to face he will resemble a beetle . . . and not [the Archbishop of Canterbury]."

John Edwards will have some explaining to do when he meets The Beetle. On the day I visited Edwards's University of Washington laboratory, the air chirped with the songs of his experimental crickets. Glacial insects are the zoology professor's first love (his E-mail name is *hardsnow*), but his scholarly research deals with the neurobiology of crickets, specifically the regeneration of the nervous system. "You take bits off crickets and they grow new parts," Edwards explains in his cheery New Zealand accent. "My interest in this alpine work is that you find creatures growing in habitats where you wouldn't expect anything to be."

Alexander von Humboldt, the founder of alpine ecology, was the first scientist to be surprised by flies and butterflies living on a snow-field at 16,000 feet during his climb of Ecuador's Mount Chimborazo in 1802. Chimborazo's bugs were later surpassed by the jumping spiders of Mount Everest, which at 22,000 feet hold title to being the highest-living organism on Earth. The spider's Latin name is *Euophrys omnisuperstes*, John Edwards told me, which translates roughly as *Being above all else*. Mount Rainier's highest creatures are harvestmen, also known as daddy longlegs, which look like spiders but technically aren't (spiders have a waist between their head and abdomen; harvestmen are the no-necks of octopedal society). Harvestmen hide in the nooks and crannies of ice and broken rock during the day, then scuttle over the tops of glaciers and snowfields to forage for food at night. What's remarkable isn't so much the altitude at which these creatures survive as the fact that food exists for them to survive on: Dinner at 10,000 feet is delivered by the wind.

Some insects, like the ice worm, can survive on the microscopic organisms that grow on the surface of Rainier's glaciers and snowfields. But most require heartier fare—the pollen, fungi, and dead bodies of their arthropod kin that arrive on the mountain wind. A strategy of mass dispersal has made insects the world's most successful organisms. Each batch of newborns hatches, then immediately takes off for parts unknown. Some ladybugs wake from winter and fly to an aphid breakfast hundreds of miles away. Infant spiders climb to the top of the nearest tree and spin strands of silk that catch the wind, a process known as ballooning. Insects can ride a good thermal across continents. Moths have been sighted more than a thousand miles at sea. Desert locusts can cross bodies of water fifteen hundred miles wide.

Hundreds of tons of European aphids blow out to the North Sea every year. On a summer day, fully half the insect world is in the air.

"We don't see them because they're too small, but there's a kind of aerial plankton up there," says John Edwards. It's a numbers game; most insects crash and die in their new homes, but four or five in a thousand may live—and that's enough to set up shop for the next generation. "They don't have much control over where they come down," says Edwards. "So if you happen to come down on a glacier, bad luck, mate!" he chuckles. Once they're blown onto the Emmons Glacier or Muir Snowfield, they're too cold to take off again, so they become reluctant entries on the day's board of fare. Aphids, ants, and more than two hundred other insect species from Eastern Washington's crop fields regularly blow up to Rainier's highest elevations; some have been found in the summit crater itself. Edwards once calculated that on a given summer day—mid-June is usually the peak—a standing twelve-ton crop of desiccating insects sits on the mountain's permanent snow.

My snowshoeing forays around Paradise became bug hunts. Since I couldn't make Skip stop for every creature that crossed the trail, I scooped them up in plastic test tubes. By the time I arrived home, though, my tube zoo had turned to bug mush. The insects couldn't stand the heat.

Springtails and other cold-hardy insects prosper in winter because they can supercool their bodies to temperatures at which others freeze and die. Most active winter bugs can supercool their bodies to a range of –6 to –12 degrees Celsius, going lower by producing more glycerol and dropping the water content in their bodies. Some insects manufacture peptides that act like organic antifreeze. Other bugs that go dormant in winter (usually burrowing under tree bark or into the ground) let parts of their bodies freeze, but control the growth of ice within each cell so that crystal spears don't puncture their cell membranes. Dormant bugs can go into a far deeper freeze than active ones; some can survive to −70 degrees Celsius, near the lowest extremes recorded on the Earth's poles.

Our notions of temperature are anthropocentric; if the thermometer indicates 10 below, we assume the whole world shivers with us. But most active winter insects live in, on, and under the snowpack in a remarkably stable and toasty microclimate. Except in the Arctic, where permafrost sits under the topsoil that thaws every summer, the ground rarely freezes. Every December the skies over Rainier insulate the mountain with a blanket of snow that stabilizes the surface of the underlying soil at temperatures ranging from 0 to −10 degrees Celsius. Ladybugs actually seek out high elevations, such as Burroughs Mountain on Rainier's northeast flank, to overwinter under the protection of the snowpack. In summer they return to the valleys to feed on aphids. The snow scorpionfly, which looks like a small mosquito without wings, spends brilliant winter days trundling over the snow, drawing energy from both the sun and its reflection on the snow surface. On bad weather days it stays three feet deep in the snowpack, where temperatures never retreat below −3 degrees Celsius even when the surface dips to 25 below.

Some winter insects are more likely to fry than freeze. Above John Edwards's desk at the University of Washington hangs a photograph of his pride and joy, a distinctly unappealing insect known as the grylloblattid. The yellow-brown crawler looks like the result of an amorous encounter between earwig and cockroach. "*Grylloblattid* means cricket-cockroach, actually," Edwards corrects me. The gryllo (for short), which exists only in the Canadian Rockies and on mountain glaciers in the Pacific Rim, was the last order of insect to be discovered by entomologists. As we spoke, in fact, Edwards's collection from Mount Rainier was at a nearby laboratory where a colleague hoped to determine whether the local gryllo deserved status as an entirely new species. Grylloblattids survive in a thin 21-degree temperature band. Below –6 degrees Celsius they freeze, but they live in and around ice that's always close to zero. "If you cup them in your hand for five minutes or so and warm them up above 15 degrees centigrade," Edwards says, "they go into heat convulsions and die."

I once tested the truth of Edwards's words by plucking a winter cranefly from the snow while skiing with Skip across Reflection Lake. The fly scrambled over a tuft of snow scooped up around it. At the edge of the snow, it extended a tentative leg onto my bare hand and flexed twice, like a man testing the strength of lake ice, before recoiling at the hot plate of my palm. As the snow turned to water and dripped through my fingers, the fly clung to the ice like a melting planet.

In our age of ecological awareness, we're constantly reminded of the interconnectedness of all life on Earth, but unacknowledged in that message are the vast distances separating the realms in which we live. The snow flea and the grylloblattid exist within such a thin strip of our own universe—between ice crystals or within the tight confines of temperature—that their presence or absence is as nothing to us. So it is with the human relation to the mountain. *Homo sapiens* thrives in such a narrow dimension of the mountain universe—in one season, on fair-weather days, with artificial goosedown and Gore-Tex skin— that we are as nothing to it.

GRIND THE MOUNTAIN'S
SHATTERED BONES

*S*pring *turned into summer by the time I faced the*
fact that the only thing keeping me from completing the
Wonderland Trail was my own fear of spending another
week in misery's attic. My tent sat in a closet, cultivating a mildewy
odor that made me wince when I opened the door. I had little desire
to resume lodging in the collapsible cell of the damned.

A change of tactics. I decided to chip away at the trail. I walked the
mountain's southern forests in one- and two-day jaunts. They passed
with sufficient pleasure that I chanced a longer trip along the mountain's northern edge. The trail from Mowich Lake edges past the terminus of the Carbon Glacier, skirts the icy pond of Mystic Lake, winds

around the butt of the Winthrop Glacier, and continues over the camelbacks of Burroughs Mountain to Sunrise. Before setting out I took a blood-racing dip in Mowich Lake, the park's largest pool. Through the calm morning water I could see a tangle of drowned trees waiting to trap my feet, but I needn't have worried. The water was so cold I never dove far below the surface. For a few seconds I floated face up, hoping to catch sight of the summit, but too many rocks and peaks obstructed the view. This wasn't unusual. The closer I got to the mountain, the more difficult it was to see.

Six miles out of Mowich Lake I caught sight of the Carbon Glacier, or what I thought must be its grey tongue rolling down the mountain's northern face. Seen from the distance of a mile, the upper Carbon Valley appeared to be filled with fading beauty bark. I followed the trail along the western bank of the Carbon River and into the heat of the day. Mosquitoes swarmed me, stabbed me, and died in the chemical slick on my neck. The Wonderland crossed the Carbon River on a steel cable suspension bridge that bounced like a trampoline when you really got the momentum going and provided a closer look at the glacier's five-story terminus wall, which now appeared to be dressed in elephant hide, all wrinkles and pocks.

Across the bridge and closer still, the ice revealed its true self. Meltwater streamed down its face into the Carbon River, brown and angry at its source. I moved down the bank, hoping to cool myself against the ice. A Park Service sign warned against it: falling rock, swift water, cave-ins. I ignored the sign and hopped down a boulder path before the sound of air cut by high-velocity motion stopped me in my tracks. I listened. More hissing. Now and then a clunk. Movement along the face caught my eye and I watched for a moment before I understood: The glacier was raining stones.

Retreating from the fire zone, I sat in the shade amid a patch of bluebells and took in the show. What I had taken for beauty bark was actually a skin of boulders.

For two hours I sat and watched rocks tumble out of the glacier. The larger ones tripped and bounded like meteors, kicking up ice spray and hitting with a fatal CHOCK! A bear cub of a boulder concussed the earth. "I've been up to the Carbon probably a dozen times," a glaciologist had told me before I set out. "The one time I broke my rule about not going too far off the trail, one of those rocks nearly killed me."

I counted the warning time someone would have from the moment a stone turned: one one thousand, two one thousand, three.

There are more than seven hundred glaciers in Washington, more than in any state but Alaska. Twenty-five are on Mount Rainier. At the snow's August ebb the glaciers cover thirty-six square miles of the mountain with an average depth of one hundred feet of ice. At its deepest point, seven hundred vertical feet of ice slide down the Carbon's bed. If you drilled the Washington Monument into the Carbon Glacier, it would stop one hundred fifty feet short of bedrock.

Rainier's northern face is dominated by the Willis Wall, a sheer 4,000-foot headwall so fearsome that park officials for years denied climbers permission to attempt it. The first ascent of the wall was accomplished only in 1961, eight years after the conquest of Everest and nearly a century after the first recorded climb of Rainier itself. The Willis Wall dumps so much shattered rock on the Carbon Glacier that the stone acts as an insulating blanket that blocks the sun's melting rays and allows the ice to flow five miles down the mountain to an elevation of 3,500 feet, the lowest reach of any glacier in the lower forty-eight states.

The Puget Sound region was once engulfed by a glacier that makes the Carbon look like pond frost. During the Pleistocene epoch, which began 1.6 million years ago and ended around 8000 B.C., massive continental glaciers advanced and retreated over the Northwest. During the last major glacial movement, about 15,000 years ago, the 3,000-foot-thick Vashon Glacier slid south from Canada to a point just past Olympia, using the depression between the Olympics and Cascades as a riverbed. "The nearest vantage point on ice-free land for an ancient citizen of Seattle would have been on Tiger Mountain or some other westerly promontory fringing the Cascades," writes naturalist Arthur Kruckeberg. "Looking westward, that person would have seen a vast sea of ice stretching without interruption to the eastern flank of the Olympic Mountains." The iceflow scoured and gouged the earth. As it retreated, its smaller impressions became Lake Washington, Lake Sammamish, and other freshwater ponds. Larger cavities were filled by the sea and became Puget Sound.

Every minute of every day the glacier grinds down the mountain, millions of grains per second. The earth moves, the wind blows, rain falls, and another slab of the Willis Wall falls down and is conveyed away by the Carbon Glacier. Underneath the freeze, rocks embedded in the ice carve deep scratches into the bedrock and let the water running around it flush out the dust. In the contest between the Earth's elements, water will vanquish rock.

The glaciers have become Rainier's neglected natural wonder, often overshadowed by the high-meadow flowers that legions of tourists come to see every summer. But earlier this century the iceflows inspired as much awe as the meadows. Here is historian Edmond Meany's 1909 paean, "Carbon Glacier":

I hail thee, river of ice and snow,
Thou source of our valleys' fertile soil.
I climb thy seamy sides to know
A tithe of thy patient, ceaseless toil.

Grind, grind, grind,
Huge stones to dust, O stream!
Grind, grind, grind,
Till thy sides as mirrors gleam!

Thy open lips of ice doth pour
A gushing stream in noisy flood,
A stream released in joyful roar,
Behold! the glacier's milk-white blood.

Grind, grind, grind,
To crumbling dust these stones!
Grind, grind, grind,
The mountain's shattered bones!

Was this great rock by Titan tossed
Thy cold, brown breast to crush and bruise;
Or didst thy maiden, wintry frost
Launch playful boat for seaward cruise?

Grind, grind, grind,
The rocks however hurled!
Grind, grind, grind,
Thou millstone of a world!

Inspired by Meany, I climbed the Carbon's seamy sides, but found nothing except loose rock and ice bridges thin enough to punch through, forcing me to abort my romantic encounter with the glacier. If you hang around up top of a glacier, you'll hear it creak and groan but won't feel it move. Down below it's tough to tell where the rocky moraine ends and the ice begins; shrubs actually grow in the soilcoat. Traversing a glacier feels like walking across a giant's body. You don't realize you're right on the old man's chest until you hear him groan. And then you want to get off him in a very bad way.

Meany's poem continues for another six stanzas before concluding in a final chorus:

> Grind, grind, grind,
> And grind exceeding fine!
> Grind, grind, grind,
> My master's will and thine!

Grind *exceeding fine!* Nature in Meany's age was bold and striking, everything a man of his day wished to be. Meany's glacier was a Teddy Roosevelt of ice.

The glacier, a symbol of roaring power and force of will in Edmond Meany's time, has become at the twentieth century's end as much an emblem of purity as the mountain itself. Beer and bottled water companies claim to pipe their water direct from the glacier's mouth. Today's beverage makers, if they cared, would be surprised to see a glacial river up close. Far from pristine, a flow like the Carbon runs coffee-brown with the flaky offscourings of the glacier's bed, and contains particles of insects, animals, and sometimes even humans whose bodies the ice has ground exceeding fine. But each age projects its desires on the far-off hills. Edmond Meany saw in the glaciers a massive power that humbled the mighty mountain. We look high and see a natural purity we're desperate to recapture.

It's easy to die on a glacier. Humans have been doing it for more than five thousand years. In 1991 two hikers in the Ötztal Alps along the Austrian-Italian border discovered the body of a man emerging from the melting ice. His skin had turned to leather, but his body and his tools were intact. After extensive testing, scientists determined that the man had perished on the ice sometime around 3200 B.C.

Most victims of a glacier fall into crevasses, deep cuts created by the pressure of moving ice. Often they're disguised by thick snowfall that forms a bridge across the gap. When these snowbridges give way, they go so quickly that climbers often call the event "popping through." Seracs, ice towers formed when the glacier moves down a particularly steep slope and breaks apart, loom above climbers. When they fall, they kill. In 1981 a serac toppled onto Mount Rainier's Ingraham Glacier and broke into huge chunks of ice. The blocks started an avalanche that engulfed a party of twenty-nine climbers making for the summit. Eleven climbers were killed in what still stands as the deadliest accident in American climbing history.

Climbing season in the Cascades runs from June to September. As the summer wears on, glaciers become scarred with crevasses. "When a glacier's in shape in June, you can just march straight up," says David McGovern, who's been guiding in the Cascades since 1972. "As the season progresses, the route becomes more serpentine. You have to end-run around one crevasse and then go around another. In June, a glacier ascent may take ten hours. By October, it might not even be possible."

If you're alone when you pop through a snowbridge, you stand a good chance of staying in the ice for ten to ten thousand years. If you're roped in, you hope your buddies plant their ice axes and hold on, stopping your fall and preventing your pulling them in like beads on a string. Recently two climbers standing next to a crevasse on the Ingraham Glacier were blown in by a sixty-mile-per-hour gust of wind. And that was in summer.

Crevasses open and close quickly. In 1991, about the time the ancient Alp walker was emerging from the ice, two climbers from Colorado, Lester Spross and James Tuttle, crossed the Ingraham Glacier on their way to the summit. Tuttle made his way across a snowbridge that held him, but which he weakened by his crossing. Spross, following, dropped through and landed on soft snow two hundred feet below. Tuttle, roped in, slowed Spross's fall but was pulled in by his own weight. He fell into a tight V-notch twenty feet above his partner. Both survived the fall, but with every breath Tuttle slipped farther down the notch. Before he suffocated he told his partner, "Don't die here with me." For two days Spross hacked at the ice, eventually filling the crevasse with enough ice and snow to climb out, using Tuttle's spiked crampons tied to his hands.

"By the time we got up there to recover the body," recalls Gus Bush, one of the Tacoma Mountain Rescue Unit volunteers who searched for Tuttle, "the crevasse had closed. Some of 'em don't have to close up much. Then comes the question: Do you want to put the rescuer's life at risk to recover the body?"

Alpine glaciers were in unusual retreat in 1991, the summer that "Ötzi," as the ice man was named, emerged from the ice. Five other bodies turned up during the season, including two climbers missing since 1934. Two others who were trapped in a crevasse in 1953 were found three hundred meters from where they had fallen. The body of another, killed in 1981, came out of the glacier three hundred fifty meters away from where he went in. The most harrowing show of glacial force, though, actually came a few years before the warm summer of 1991. From 1985 to 1990 the body of a man killed at the end of the sixteenth century was recovered in an Alpine glacier. The recovery process took five years, because he turned up in pieces that were scattered over a seventy-five-meter area.

The seed of these billion-pound ice cubes we call glaciers is a single snowflake. A frozen six-pointed crystal floats to earth and joins uncountable others in a puffy fill that's something like ten percent ice, ninety percent air. Then the flakes begin to lose their points. Air moving through the pile turns some to water vapor, which refreezes; others melt under the pressure of the next snowfall. After about a year the snow turns to firn (also called névé), a kind of corn snow with crystals the size of Chiclets. Three to five years of pressurized refreezing eventually turn the firn into dense glacial ice.

Glaciers form when more snow falls in winter than melts away in summer. The weight of the accumulating ice and snow forces the pack to move, which it does via the path of least resistance: down the mountain. Above a glacier's equilibrium line, snow survives the summer thaw and manufactures more ice. Below it, the ice begins the glacier's long, slow melt.

The ice doesn't so much run down the mountain as skate. Hockey players glide because the friction created by their metal blades melts the ice beneath it; in effect, they're skimming on a thin line of water. A glacier moves similarly. Water running between the ice and bedrock allows the glacier to slide across the rock.

Ice also flows within the glacier itself, as some crystals slip past others. Like water in a river, ice flows faster on top and in the center, where there's less friction to slow it down. If you planted five stakes straight across a glacier and loosely connected them with rope, in a few weeks the rope would form a smile. The Nisqually Glacier, which terminates a few hundred yards east of Paradise, moves about eight to eighteen inches a day, although researchers have recorded abnormally thick sections moving faster than seventy-two inches a day.

In the 1840s the Nisqually Glacier reached about nine hundred feet past the Nisqually River bridge on the Paradise Road. Today the terminus sits more than a mile upvalley. The Carbon is currently in mild retreat; the ice at the terminus is melting back faster than the motion of the glacier can push it ahead. It has shrunk twenty feet every year since 1986.

A light breeze kicked up and reminded me that I still had a long walk to Mystic Lake. I relaced my boots, balanced The Renegade's load, checked my map, and broke into a king-size Baby Ruth. Before leaving the Carbon for the three-mile incline, I sat and watched the river carry the mountain away. Glacial flour turned the water to chocolate milk.

The river ran so fiercely you could hear rocks tumbling over one another. I cupped a handful of water and let it drain through my fingers. Specks of dark andesite caught in the ridges of my skin. I scooped another handful, brought it to my lips, and drank the mountain down.

VOLCANO

There once was a Civilian Conservation Corps camp at Sunrise, and you can't help but envy the army of young bachelors who lived here on FDR's dime. With shovels and picks the CCC established a ranger station and visitor center at the 6,000-foot-high alpine park. Sunrise is the mountain's undiscovered Elysium, so snowbound and remote that it stays closed all but eight weeks of the year. When Rainier climbing guides want to show visiting relatives the mountain, they leave Paradise and drive to Sunrise.

On a clear late-summer night, I drove to Sunrise to finish off the Wonderland. At two-thirty in the morning five cars and a camper slept under a candent quarter moon. A cool breeze, the dead of night. Stars pitted the black bowl of sky. I turned the headlights off and let my eyes adjust to the dim world of shadow and form. The stone visitor's lodge, the restrooms, the drinking fountain, the gift shop. With just enough light in the sky, I strapped on the loaded Renegade and followed the trail down the eastern side of Mount Rainier.

The mountain rarely went completely dark. Against the black sky Rainier's ice accepted the moonlight and turned luminous, becoming a dimmer moon on the horizon. Stumbling over roots and rocks, I closed the distance between us. Points of light pricked the Emmons Glacier, signals from headlamped climbers already an hour into their summit day.

Hiking at night liberates the secondary senses from the dominance of sight. The air swirls with sensuous streams and eddies—the sweet lift of pine scent, the dewy fragrance of a mountain meadow, crickets chirring in and out of my ears. As the trail crossed a chattering creek, ribbons of cool air curled around my forearms, raising goosebumps. The radiant stones of a rockslide warmed the draft and chased the pimples away.

At a viewpoint I sat and watched the light come home. Stars slipped away and color leaked into the world: lavender aster, yellow daisy, deep blue lupine. Near dawn I wore a hat and two pairs of gloves; it's still cold up this high. A whine annoyed my ear; the bugs were stirring. A few minutes after their awakening, as if roused by the buzzing of breakfast, Steller's jays and rosy finches gave full-throated greetings to the day.

I rose and brushed a layer of fine dust off my butt. I was surprised, because dust is as uncommon as cactus on the mountain's wet western side. I picked up a stone and recognized the pocked surface of pumice. Under the heel of my boot it reverted to dust. I found another and pocketed it and walked east toward the summit. In my notebook I jotted a word: Volcano.

Science isn't truth, it's merely our best stab at it. At the heart of scientific inquiry lies its thrilling contingency, the possibility that today's crackpot theory may be tomorrow's natural law. In the study of mountains, the force behind their creation—tectonic motion—has become accepted only in the last thirty years. As recently as the early 1960s, the theory of continental drift was considered so ludicrous that geology professors included it in their lectures on daffy moments in earth science. On Mount Rainier, geologists are just now discovering what the mountain is made of, how it was formed, and when it rose from the earth.

In the beginning there was no mountain at all. Sixty million years ago, geologists believe, the area around Mount Rainier was a broad lowland of swamps and deltas on the margin of the Pacific Ocean. If you stood on the present site of Rainier and looked west, you might have seen volcanic islands poking through the sea; to the east the land lapsed into the horizon as level as a plain. Twenty million years later volcanoes rose on the flatlands around the current national park and became islands as the region sank and the sea rushed in. During the next twenty-five million years immense floods of liquid basalt poured out of vents in the Blue Mountains near present-day Spokane and covered Eastern Washington, Oregon, and parts of Idaho, Nevada, and Northern California under one of the world's largest lava formations.

Some flows ran all the way to the Pacific Ocean before the North American and Pacific plates collided and threw up the Cascade Range to block them.

Nonvolcanic mountains rise up when continental plates crash into one another, much as the hoods of two cars accordion in a head-on. The African plate rammed into the Eurasian plate and up sprang the Alps. The Himalayas were born of the cataclysmic union of the Eurasian and Indian plates. The Pacific plate, which underlies the Pacific Ocean and a precarious section of California, is currently slipping past the North American plate, which underlies the continent and half the Atlantic Ocean. The Pacific moves north, the North American plate moves south, and the stress that builds between them is relieved by earthquakes along their border: the San Andreas Fault.

If you plotted all the significant earthquakes of the past century and all the volcanic eruptions of the past ten thousand years on a world map, you'd find yourself staring at a connect-the-dots puzzle that revealed the Earth's dozen or so major tectonic plates. The dots would be so thick around the Pacific plate that they'd barely leave room for a connecting line. This is the well-known "Ring of Fire" that encircles the Pacific Ocean from southern Chile to the Aleutian Islands, Japan, the Philippines, and New Zealand: where the massive Pacific plate has collided with seven others and given rise to half the world's active volcanoes.

Mount Rainier sits in the middle of the Ring of Fire. The mountain exists because of the Juan de Fuca plate, a jagged little piece caught between the jaws of the Pacific and the North American plates. The Juan de Fuca runs about fifty miles offshore from Northern California to the northern tip of Vancouver Island, is about two hundred fifty miles wide at its broadest point, and resembles a saw with three teeth pointed west. The Juan de Fuca and Pacific plates are diverging—tearing apart from each other at a rate of six centimeters per year. The Juan de Fuca and North American plates converge at a rate of four centimeters per year, which is approximately twice the velocity of a growing fingernail. Because the oceanic plate is denser than the continental plate, instead of ramming into each other and thrusting up another Himalayan range the Juan de Fuca plate dives, or subducts, under the North American plate and creates a deep oceanic trench off the Washington coast. From there the subducting plate sinks into the Earth's interior but doesn't disappear completely. As it approaches the hot asthenosphere, the plate partially melts into magma, which begins to seep up through the North American plate and eventually emerges as volcanic andesite more than one hundred miles inland in the bowels of Mount Rainier.

Rainier is a recent arrival on the scene. The volcano's foundation of mile-deep granodiorite pushed through the bedrock about twelve million years ago. A close cousin of granite, salt-and-peppery-looking granodiorite resembles a Jackson Pollock canvas. You can still find quarries of it at the foot of Unicorn Peak in the Tatoosh Range along the southern border of Mount Rainier National Park. Nothing over-topped the granodiorite until about 500,000 years ago when thick lava burbled up through a vent in the bedrock and spoked out five to fifteen miles in all directions, creating the first nub of Rainier. The fresh extrusion was andesite, the world's second most common volcanic rock (after basalt), a dull grey stone that acquired its name from South America's Andes mountains. Shoulders of andesite grew into ridges as fresh rock poured over previous flows, and eventually acquired names like Rampart Ridge, which casts its afternoon shadow over Longmire; and Burroughs Mountain, the double hump that runs from the Winthrop Glacier to Sunrise. Occasional volcanic explosions threw plumes of ash and pumice into the air; westerly winds sweeping in from the Pacific carried them to the eastern side of the mountain, where they settled in dry saffron-and-olive pools near the heel of Burroughs Mountain. In *The Geologic Story of Mount Rainier*, a guidebook I picked up at the Paradise gift shop, geologist Dwight Crandell explains it like this: "As the volcano matured, the long thick flows were succeeded by thinner and shorter ones which, piled on top of one another, built the giant cone that now dominates the region." The latest radiometric studies of Rainier's oldest rocks dates them back 496,000 years, which puts the mountain in line with its southern Cascadian neighbors. Mount Adams is 560,000 years old; Mount Hood was created sometime around 600,000 years ago. (It would be convenient if the Cascade volcanoes lined up according to age like geologic Von Trapps, but they don't. Mount St. Helens, the youngest, rises between Hood and Adams.)

Tom Sisson, a geologist mapping the volcanic structure of Rainier, told me how the hot andesite built up ridges instead of running into the mountain's valleys. "A lot of these ridges formed during the ice ages," he explained. "Imagine filling all the existing valleys with ice, then sending lava flows out along the margins of those glaciers. When the flow hits the ice it hardens and creates a dam, so instead of flowing onto the glacier it continues down the ridge. When the ice age ends, the glaciers melt away and you get pretty much what you see now."

Sisson's own detective work had revealed this scenario. On the margin of the ridges he found a lot of glassy sections of rock, which indicated that the magma cooled very, very quickly. In some places it was a meter thick, and "to chill the molten part of the magma to glass, you've got to chill it pretty darn fast," he said. That meant the magma hit something colder than water: ice.

Since 1992 Sisson had spent his summers mapping the 14,410-foot volcano, every ridge and valley, using only a clipboard, a pencil, and a magnifying glass. A typical week saw him hike into the backcountry and spend four days analyzing rocks and collecting samples on an 11,000-foot ridge. After four days Sisson and his assistant hiked out with backpacks full of rocks. Over the winter he sorted through the samples at his U.S. Geological Survey (USGS) office in Menlo Park, California. He sent some to a laboratory for radiometric dating; others he melted at high pressure to reproduce the conditions under which the original magma formed, which might eventually tell him why the volcano erupted the way it did.

To understand how young Mount Rainier is, geologically speaking, imagine the last sixty million years compressed into a week that begins at 12:01 Monday morning. Around the mountain the week is largely uneventful. Monday, Tuesday, Wednesday, Thursday, Friday pass; nothing happens. A few minutes past noon on Saturday, granodiorite pours out of the ground. Half a world away, the earliest *Homo sapiens* show up in Africa around 6:00 Sunday night. At 10:30 Sunday night the volcano begins to rise, and completes its cone at twenty-two seconds before midnight—twenty-two hundred years ago.

Most people who live around the mountain don't like to think about it, but the bare fact is that Mount Rainier is the most dangerous volcano in the United States of America. That doesn't mean it is the most likely to erupt (it isn't), or that it has the deadliest history (it doesn't), or that the day after tomorrow it might go off like Mount St. Helens (it won't). What that means is that on the matrix of human population and catastrophic event, Mount Rainier sits at the top of the chart. More people in the state of Washington live around a dangerous mountain than do people anywhere else in the country. The more scientists learn about Mount Rainier, the more nervous they become, because in the last few years they've discovered that the danger doesn't lie, as they thought earlier, in a volcanic eruption. What's got the geologists spooked is the fact that the mountain could collapse at any minute.

For decades geologists reassured the residents of Puget Sound that Rainier was a dormant, not an extinct, volcano. That meant it wasn't dead, just sleeping. But the degree of reassurance delivered by the term "dormant" depended on one's definition of dormancy. Some geologists consider any volcano active in the last ten thousand years to be an "active" volcano. Rainier's last eruption took place less than one hundred fifty years ago, which in geological terms is like late last night. Since the 1870s, mountain climbers had reported a high degree of geothermal activity within the crater; that is, the mountain blew off a lot of steam. Although the mountain has long drawn the attention of explorers, climbers, painters, and poets, for volcanologists Mount Rainier has been something of a bore. With more than fifty volcanoes erupting around the world every year, few earth scientists wanted to waste their careers studying a peak so inaccessible and, in geological terms, dull. "When Rainier's been active, it's not been an explosive volcano," said USGS geologist Kevin Scott. "It's really been sort of a wimp."

That attitude changed on May 18, 1980, when Mount St. Helens erupted and triggered massive avalanches, debris flows, and ashfall that killed fifty-seven people. Cascade volcanoes became hot scientific property. Because the scientists' geological problems were now life- and property-threatening issues, politicians became interested, which meant government funding. It's difficult to overstate the importance of St. Helens to volcanic research. Recent American earth science is now divided into epochs: Before St. Helens and After St. Helens. "A lot of people who were involved with the successful prediction of [the erup- tion of the Philippine volcano] Pinatubo in 1991 cut their teeth on data from St. Helens," one seismologist told me. He could have been talking about any geologist or seismologist in America.

Since 1970 scientists have kept watch over a network of seis- mometers around Rainier and other Cascade volcanoes. Their vigi- lance, and the number of seismometers, increased significantly after the eruption of Mount St. Helens, since seismic activity around the volcano—there were more than ten thousand earthquakes in the eight weeks leading up to the eruption—was the most obvious sign that it was about to blow.

From his office at the University of Washington, seismologist Steve Malone can call up today's activity at Mount Rainier with a few strokes of his computer keyboard. If the mountain begins to grow restless, Malone will be the first person in the world to know it. What he looks for are changes in the size, number, type, and location of earthquakes around the mountain. Like a Secret Service officer, Malone looks for anything out of the ordinary. On the day I visited, the data revealed no assassins in the crowd.

That Malone and his colleagues have this data at their fingertips "doesn't mean we can sit here and tell you Mount Rainier is going to erupt in three years," he said. "It does mean that if the mountain were to erupt in the next month or two, we should see precursors. We're continuously monitoring Mount Rainier as well as the other Cascade volcanoes so that when the eruption comes—I don't say if, I say when—we will be able to anticipate it and give a warning that, Okay, stuff is changing, it's on the way.

"At this point all we can say is it would be *highly* unlikely that the mountain would erupt in the next few weeks. But a longer period than that, who knows? It could be months, it could be years, it could be decades."

Faults are rock fractures. They range from localized fissures a hundred yards long to continental monsters like the San Andreas. One of the larger Pacific Northwest faults runs for nearly fifty miles and passes directly under Mount St. Helens. "There may be an offset or a kink right around where the mountain is, which may in fact be *why* Mount St. Helens is there," Malone explained. A slight change in angle in a fault system can generate a tensional zone (where the rock pulls apart), which allows magma to rise up through the crust. But because Mount Rainier is not Mount St. Helens, if you ask Steve Malone where the kink lies in Rainier's basement, he will tell you he doesn't know.

He knows *some* kind of fault is rocking the mountain, because his equipment records around one hundred thirty low-level earthquakes there every year, which makes it by far the most seismically active Cascade volcano. During the 1980s the university's seismometers worked overtime recording the endless series of quakes at Mount St. Helens, whose number Malone quantified technically as "a jillion." Activity has quieted significantly since the mid-1990s, and now St. Helens experiences about fifty in an average year. California's Lassen Peak, which erupted dramatically between 1914 and 1917, follows Rainier with about one hundred yearly quakes.

A word of advice: When speaking with a seismologist, erase the term "Richter scale" from your vocabulary. Charles Richter was the CalTech seismologist who created the scale of earthquake magnitude in 1935. To a seismologist, the Loma Prieta earthquake that disrupted the 1989 World Series in San Francisco was a magnitude 7.1 event. If you say, as I did, "Seven-point-one on the Richter scale," seismologists will chuckle at your naiveté. "When I ask a seismologist friend of mine to define the Richter scale," Steve Malone told me, "his definition is: What the press calls magnitude." Malone repeated the phrase to himself, "On the 'Richter' scale," and laughed. Repeat after me: Magnitude.

I found Seth Moran in a basement office next to the seismology lab. Moran, a PhD candidate working under Steve Malone, was completing an ambitious map of the faults around the Mount Rainier section of the Cascades using technology derived from medical CAT scans, which feeds X-ray data into a computer to produce an anatomical cross-section. Instead of X-rays, Moran used the seismic waves generated by naturally occurring earthquakes to form a similar cross-section of the Earth, which might reveal what the area's underlying layers of rock are made of and where the big cracks lie. Sporting the uniform of the geology graduate student—Hawaiian print shirt, khaki shorts, low-maintenance beard, Oberlin Earth Day coffee mug—Moran accompanied me to the lab and walked me through the various events recorded by the mountain's four seismometers, which are planted at Longmire, on Mount Fremont, and at the two high climbing camps,

Camp Muir and Camp Schurman. A handwritten legend sitting atop the machines interpreted the language of the helicorder drum:

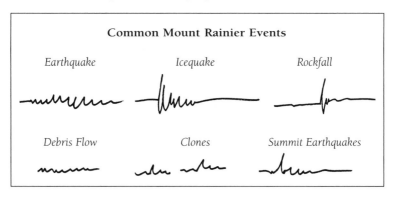

I asked Moran what a clone was, and he said nobody knew. "They're these small events that happen fairly close to one another, and they're identical. They appear out of nowhere and then disappear." We watched the Schurman seismograph squiggle out the minor pops and grinds of the Emmons Glacier, and every once in a while we'd see a mysterious series of growing spikes and a slam, then nothing for a minute or two before the series reversed—a slam and a series of fading spikes. Moran interpreted.

"It's right next to the outhouse up at Camp Schurman," he told me. "It took us a while to figure that out."

Of the many possible scenarios in which Mount Rainier visits destruction upon the people living beneath it, the worst would bring twenty feet of mud roaring through the farm town of Orting, Washington, at thirty miles per hour. Orting sits in a quiet mountain valley between Tacoma and Mount Rainier. On a clear day the volcano looms above the 2,960 residents of the little town like an enormous white wart. Geologists, who like to keep people from dying in volcanic disasters, have lately descended on Orting to figure out a way to warn the residents when disaster is about to strike, because lately they've discovered that every five hundred years or so, a massive chunk of Mount Rainier collapses and triggers a mudflow that inundates the valley below. And underlying the foundation of every house in Orting is a mudflow that's five hundred fifty years old.

Orting's sitting-duck position became known when Kevin Scott, a hydrology expert who'd studied the mudflows triggered by Mount St. Helens, investigated an event known as the Electron Mudflow. A half-century before Columbus set sail for America, a massive chunk of Mount Rainier peeled off and buried the Orting valley in fifteen feet of former summit. The existence of the Electron had already been established; what Scott discovered was that the mudflow came unaccompanied by volcanic activity. By comparing the dates of other flows around Rainier, Scott determined that flows the size of the Electron happened about once every five hundred years. In sporting terms, Orting was due.

If the mountain collapsed, Scott figured it would take less than an hour for the slurry to reach the Orting valley and fan out over its farms and tract houses. Once it hit town it would take less than a minute for the death muck to turn Cope's Pharmacy, the Spar Pole Pub, American Legion Post 167, the Timber Tavern, the Park Bench Cafe, the Bank of Sumner, the Exxon station, the Orting Food Center, and Orting High School, home of the mighty Cardinals, into topsoil. I asked Scott if it would be anything like the North Fork Toutle flow that followed the eruption of St. Helens, the one in the film clip where the floating house disintegrates when it hits the bridge. "Think of that as a much smaller version of what we're talking about here," he said.

Mount Rainier is a volcano with an active hydrothermal system, which means the mountain cooks its rocks in acidic water twenty-four hours a day every day, every week, every year. Inside the mountain centuries of steam heat turn hard andesite into gooey clay. While this chemistry project goes on inside, thirty-six square miles of ice grinds away at the mountain's ridges. Water seeps into every crack of every wall and freezes overnight, expanding and fracturing the stone. Rocks shatter and yield to gravity's call; the mountain never stops falling apart.

Clay has a relatively low coefficient of viscosity. That is, it wants to flow. If a chunk of Mount Rainier collapsed, the clay wouldn't stop when it hit the glaciers.

"That landslide would be so saturated that it would run like water all the way to Puget Sound," explained Scott. Public officials planning for the big flow are confronted with the concept of "channel roughness," which holds that a fluid moves faster over a smoother surface. Previous mudflows from Mount Rainier ran through valleys studded with old-growth Douglas fir. Today the Orting valley sits level, plowed, and planted with row crops. "The expression 'Slick as snot' occurs to me," one geologist said.

If you park your car and walk around Orting, you can find evidence of the mountain's destructive potential. On the margin between the valley's remaining farms and the creeping suburbia of housing developments are fields pebbled with andesite boulders, some of them five feet across, brought down from on high. A Volvo-size boulder of volcanic breccia, a cluster of sharp-angled rocks that flowed in on the Electron, rests next to a new housing subdivision. Contractors digging housing foundations unearthed an old-growth Douglas fir forest buried by the flow. Some of the trees, which sprouted about the time William the Conqueror charged across England, were so well preserved they could have been sold for lumber.

If geologists can figure out what triggered the Electron, they might be able to give the residents of Orting time to escape the wall of mud. Their best guess is that a massive section of the mountain near the Sunset Amphitheater (the high cirque that forms the headwall of the Puyallup Glacier) slid away from the volcano, which might account for the depression that forms the Amphitheater. Flows like the Electron are technically called "lahars" because "mudflow" is too inaccurate, mud being only one of many ingredients in the flow. The word originated in Indonesia, where lahars are notorious hazards. In 1919 the Javanese volcano Kelut erupted and spilled thirty-nine million cubic yards of water from its crater lake. As it fell the water picked up loose rocks and soil, creating a lahar that damaged or destroyed one hundred four villages and killed fifty-five hundred people.

Their predictions of impending doom don't exactly endear the USGS to the people of Orting. An official from the Pierce County Economic Development Board once called Kevin Scott for advice. "We need to tell people in these mudflow channels what types of buildings to construct," he told the geologist. "What's going to resist one of these big flows?" Scott thought for a moment and replied, "Nothing." When Pierce County government officials asked him to define the statistical probability of a lahar running through the valley, he delivered the news this way: "Look, the risk of a building being destroyed by a lahar from Mount Rainier within those hazard zones is greater than the risk of damage or destruction of that building by fire." On the day he showed me around Orting, Scott left his USGS-marked vehicle at the office.

Scott works out of the Cascades Volcano Observatory (CVO), which isn't a classic "observatory" but a two-story office complex in Vancouver, Washington. The USGS established the CVO to monitor the Cascade volcanoes after the eruption of Mount St. Helens. Mementos of Scott's trade are strewn around his office: an REI ice axe, posters of Oregon's Crater Lake and New Zealand's Mount Ruapehu, a map of Mount Rainier's mudflows, and a banner from the Rotary Club of the Philippine city of Angeles, a souvenir from the Pinatubo years. "Let me dig out some pictures," Scott said. He rummaged through some papers on his desk. "Here they are. This is a lahar that came down the Rio Paez, in central Colombia, in 1994, from a volcano called Nevado del Huila." The picture showed a muddy river running through a grassy pasture. "This is where the town used to be." The slurry came so fast, he said, that it overtook a man on a galloping horse. Seventeen hundred people died. He flipped to the next picture. "Here's a substantial stone masonry structure." The photo showed a field of rubble.

The Nevado del Huila lahar enacted Scott's worst fears about Rainier, because it happened while the volcano was quiet. "This thing was seismically triggered," he said. "Which shows that an earthquake can trigger a deadly flow that literally comes out of nowhere." An earthquake brought the hillside down, and the rumblings of the lahar were so similar to aftershocks that the villagers didn't pay them any mind. "They didn't know the flow was coming until it came racing around the curved river channel," Scott said. "It engulfed them seconds after they saw it. There was no time to escape."

Steve Malone's data on Rainier's seismic activity did nothing to allay Kevin Scott's concerns. The mountain's high degree of activity relative to other Cascade volcanoes, combined with the emerging data on past flank collapses, led to a bit of alarm among geologists. The possibility that an earthquake or steam explosion could trigger a lahar on the order of the Electron put Scott and his colleagues in a difficult position: an eruption they could predict; a flank collapse they couldn't. All they could do was study the aftermath of events like the Electron and del Huila disaster and hope they could crack the mystery of the mountain before the mountain cracked down on Orting.

In his 1620 treatise *Novum Organum*, Francis Bacon observed the curious similarity between the shape of the South American coast and the western outline of Africa. The two coasts fit together like pieces of a torn page, a fact that eventually led to the theory of continental drift, the idea that the planet's land masses were once joined in a supercontinent before breaking apart and drifting to their current locations.

In 1896 the American geologist Israel Russell looked at Mount Rainier in the way Francis Bacon had looked at the globe. He saw a conical volcano flawed by a jagged cut at the top, and imagined a puzzle with a missing piece: the summit.

Mount Rainier may have reached its greatest height more than fifty-seven hundred years ago when, some geologists suspect, the peak topped out at more than 16,000 feet. By projecting the mountain's ridgelines to an imaginary apex, geologists estimate the original peak may have once topped out nearly two thousand feet above the current summit.

Some scientists are dubious of the Great 16,000 theory. "We don't know that the mountain was ever grossly higher than it is now," Tom Sisson argued. "That 16,000 number presumes that this was once a pointy volcano. We don't know that. The only Cascade volcanoes with pointy tops are Hood, Jefferson, and, formerly, St. Helens. The rest are fairly rounded humps. The 16,000 figure *might* be true, but it's by no means fact." Despite Sisson's reservations, I chose to believe in the Great 16,000. It cast the mountain as an ancient ruin, the rubbly remnant of a giant whose dimensions took form in my imagination just as, in the mind of every classicist who traveled there, the Colossus bestrode the harbor at Rhodes.

I saw the ghost of the former mountain during my walk across the mountain's eastern hip. Over morning coffee near Sunrise, the clouds that were wadded up around the peak blew away to reveal the mountain, whole for the first time in three days. Cupping my hand, I tried to imagine what Israel Russell saw a century earlier. At arm's length, my fingers an inverted V, I connected the angles of Liberty Ridge and Gibraltar Rock at a point high above Rainier's crown. The sun flared off the Emmons Glacier and made me squint. The features of my hand formed the outline of the Great 16,000: from Gib Rock up the palm to the heart line, the dip of the crater suggested by the callus on the interdigital pad, then a slide down the pinkie finger to Liberty Cap, the eastern fall line broken only by the slight crests of the phalangeal creases. In the airspace between the mountain and my hand, you could put houses, stadiums, small towns. You could fit an entire other mountain. Where on earth did it go?

Russell thought it might have been blown off by a volcanic explosion. Other geologists later suggested that the summit was removed piecemeal through a series of small eruptions, or subsided back into the underlying magma, or was destroyed by glacial erosion. Then, in 1953, while working on a mapping project east of Tacoma, a geologist named Dwight Crandell began testing an outrageous theory: nearly six thousand years ago the summit slid off and became one of the largest mudflows in the world. Crandell's finding became known as the Osceola Mudflow, one of the geological discoveries of the century.

At the time Crandell, who goes by the name Rocky, was a thirty-year-old geologist beginning his career with the USGS. After serving with a combat infantry division in Europe, he rode the GI Bill through a small Illinois college and into the graduate geology department at Yale. The U.S. Geological Survey, which is called "The Survey" by those who work for it and "USGS" by those who don't, hired him fresh out of school. On one of his first assignments, Crandell met Howard "Hank" Waldron, who was mapping the geology of the Seattle-Tacoma region. Waldron invited Crandell to join the project and assigned him a two-hundred-square-mile section east of Tacoma.

"During the first month or so of fieldwork, I was totally perplexed by the [ancient glacial] deposit that Bailey Willis had named Osceola till ['till' is a technical term for the deposit formed at the base of a glacier]," Crandell recalled. Willis, whose namesake is the Willis Wall, completed the first geologic map of eastern Mount Rainier in 1898. In that year, Willis suggested that the till was formed by a lobe of a fifteen-thousand-year-old ice-age glacier that originated in the Cascades and merged with the Vashon ice sheet advancing into the Puget Sound region from Canada. Since the smaller glacier would have underlain the Vashon, so would its till, which Willis named "Osceola" after a nearby hamlet that dried up a few years later.

Crandell ran into problems from the start. Most glaciers deposit dirt and boulders in hummocky mounds, but the Osceola till was flat. Crandell found air pockets that looked like molds of rotted plants. Trees and stumps were trapped in the mix. Don Mullineaux, mapping the area just north of Crandell, was running across the same thing. They compared notes and found that the clayey deposit covered tens of square miles. Crandell then discovered road cuts that indicated the Osceola deposit overlay a soil on the Vashon till, which in turn indicated that time had passed between the formation of the two deposits. The "till" was younger than Willis had imagined.

"One evening I sat at my desk and considered all the modes of transportation and deposition I could think of to see which was consistent with the Osceola," Crandell recalled. "Was it really a strange glacial deposit? A river deposit? Could it have *flowed* into place? I thought of the features I had seen, and they all seemed to add up to a mudflow.

"I got pretty excited about this—in fact, my notebook includes a drawing of a light bulb."

The mudflow worked well in theory, but Crandell needed hard data. The next summer he and Hank Waldron chased the Osceola across Pierce County. They spent weeks digging holes and scraping down streambanks and road cuts, recording the thickness and composition of the mudflow. They followed it up the White River valley past the Mud Mountain Dam and Deadman Flat, and into Mount Rainier National Park. Crandell and Waldron then strapped on backpacks and traced the Osceola deposit up the side of the volcano to the top of 9,700-foot-high Steamboat Prow, a rocky wedge that cleaves the ice running from the summit into the Emmons and Winthrop Glaciers. At that point the mudflow disappeared under the glaciers.

"This led to the conclusion that the mudflow started as a massive landslide of clayey rock from the upper part of the volcano," Crandell recalled, "which was so big and fluid that it traveled at least one hundred miles before stopping in the Puget Sound lowland." Radiocarbon dating of wood mixed in the deposit put its age at roughly five thousand years. During his later studies of volcanic ash, Don Mullineaux found evidence of explosive eruptions at about the same time that the Osceola occurred, leading Crandell to link the massive mudflow with the missing summit.

Shortly after Crandell and Waldron published their findings in the June 1956 issue of the *American Journal of Science*, a group of curious geologists came out for a look. "After a day in the field one of them told me, 'There's no question in my mind that you are right, Rocky, because it is such an outrageous hypothesis that I know you have gone to great lengths to test it. But I'll be suspicious of the *next* two or three mudflows you claim to discover.'"

Glacier Basin lies directly below Steamboat Prow on the northeastern side of the mountain. It's five miles down the Wonderland Trail from Sunrise, and three miles from the popular car campground at White River. Climbers often camp here before ascending the Inter Glacier to Camp Schurman at Steamboat Prow. The Basin is a demure park whose grasses taper into sheer ridges rising a thousand feet in the sky. Fifty-seven hundred years ago a camper at Glacier Basin would have looked up to see the mountain falling on top of him.

The spoor of the Osceola still remains about a mile east of Glacier Basin along a bank of the Inter Fork of the White River. Across the trail a seventy-five-foot cliff of dried mud drops into the Inter Fork. To most hikers it's just another river cut; to geologists it's a revelation. Except for a thin bottom layer, the entire bank flowed through here in a matter of seconds. A boulder the size of a Volkswagen juts out where it was trapped five thousand years ago. I had hiked by that cliff a half-dozen times before realizing I had been strolling past the Osceola's corpse. The next time I hiked into the Basin, I took its full measure and it stole my breath. The high bank didn't even approximate the full height of the flow; it was only what stayed behind while the rest of the mountain kept going.

The massive slide split apart at the Burroughs Mountain and came back together near the present town of Greenwater; then it funneled west down the White River valley toward Puget Sound. Forty miles from the mountain, the Osceola passed through the gorge now blocked by the Mud Mountain Dam and filled it to a depth of 450 feet. To see how high 450 feet was, I hopped an elevator in downtown Seattle and got off when my altimeter registered 450. I was on the thirty-eighth floor.

On it poured, over the current sites of Buckley and Enumclaw, before splitting again. One arm inundated the valley where Auburn and Kent now lie, while another overran what's now Sumner and Puyallup before roaring past the current site of the Tacoma Dome and expiring in Commencement Bay. The Osceola carried more than 2.6 billion cubic yards of clay, silt, rock, and sand, ten times the volume of the Electron. Its size, wrote Dwight Crandell, "surpassed that of anything before or since."

Of all the ancient mountain theories my favorite is the egg axiom. Legends found in Persian, Egyptian, Greek, and Asian traditions held that the Earth was born ovoid and without blemish, bald as an egg. Ancient Jewish and Christian accounts claim God ordered the valleys to sink and mountains to rise in order to give the waters of Noah's flood somewhere to run. In other accounts, God punished the Earth for humanity's sin by raising the blemish of the continental ranges. The most fanciful theory was proposed by Ristoro d'Arezzo, an Italian metallurgist and astronomer who published his ideas in 1282. According to d'Arezzo, mountains were drawn up by the attraction of the stars, much as a magnet draws iron. The heavens themselves were full of mountains and valleys, he reasoned, the topography of which they reproduced on the land beneath them. Distant stars raised higher mountains; nearer bodies drew up gentler hills. The effect, wrote geological historian Frank Dawson Adams, "is exactly that which is produced on a level surface of wax when a seal is pressed upon it."

In d'Arezzo's conception the greater virtue of the heavens attracted the Earth. In this, the thirteenth-century Italian shared the belief of many early mountain theorists that the struggle between good and evil was made manifest in the topography of the Earth. From the early Christian theologians to Thomas Burnet's seventeenth-century *Sacred Theory of the Earth*, mountains were portrayed as deformities suffered by the land as punishment for the sins of man. Mountains were scars left after the Flood, to remind us of the moment when the world's wickedness became too much for God to bear.

Some days I drove to White River or Paradise and walked into the hills to listen to the mountain fall down. From the far field of Seattle, Mount Rainier assumes an aspect of stony permanence, but up there, close to the bone, the mountain reveals the truth of its fractured self. Slip across the broken plates of Mount Fremont, listen to the rockfall above the Nisqually Glacier, push through the sandy pumice of Burroughs Mountain; do all this and know that Mount Rainier sits above us a pile of shattered rock surrendering minute by minute to the inexorable seduction of gravity. Among the ancient Greek philosophers were some who believed the action of erosion by water proved that the Earth had not existed forever; if it had, mountains would have long since eroded into plains. This is how I think of Mount Rainier, not as an icon of permanence but as a source of relentless change, a mountain forever falling.

MARMOTA

ack on the trail. No matter how fast I hiked, I couldn't shake the marmot. He popped out of a woodpile at Sunrise, rooted through my gear at Glacier Basin, and shadowed me down the Wonderland to Summerland and Indian Bar. There wasn't just one marmot, of course, but the critters popped up so often I began to think of them as a single superagile varmint. Hoary marmots, which resemble woodchucks, aren't Rainier's most common high-altitude mammals (ground squirrels and chipmunks outnumber them), but they're one of the mountain's most fascinating creatures. They survive all year in places where bears, elk, and even mountain goats go only during summer. Their piercing alarm cries can make passing hikers jump straight into the air. And, let's face it, they're cute. A marmot's life consists of fattening up to hibernate during the harsh winter, and then hibernating. It's the kind of life I think humans would lead if we tried to live this high. We'd spend our time getting warm, finding food, repairing storm damage, and sleeping through the winter.

My favorite marmot ground was a flower field at Glacier Basin where the lupine, aster, sedges, and grass formed a courtyard bordered by the infant White River and Burroughs Mountain. At the edge of the field sat a boulder to which an early twentieth-century prospector had taken a chisel and inscribed:

MRMCO
LP

Thus was the claim of the Mount Rainier Mining Company, Limited Partnership, marked and protected. Underneath the boulder are at least two entrances to an elaborate system of burrows: marmot homes. There may be more entrances, but every time I combed the long grass I got the willies and imagined a startled hoary sinking its not-inconsiderably-sized incisors into my calf. Which, an amused marmot expert later told me, was about as likely as being struck by lightning on a clear day.

Watching a marmot is like accompanying a parent to work. You think it's going to be much more exciting than it actually is, and by midmorning you find yourself whining, "Is this all you *do* all day?" Because what marmots do all day is eat. Since they're vegetarians, and wild lupine doesn't move, the thrill of the hunt isn't part of their morning routine. There is, however, the thrill of being the *hunted.* Golden eagles, coyotes, and mountain lions eye the marmot's fatty little body like a tasty mountain snack. Since marmots' only defense is a fleet dash into the nearest burrow, they never stray far and always eat with their guard up. On slow afternoons I placed bets with myself on which marmot was most likely to be eaten by sundown.

In the late afternoon an adult male popped up from beneath the boulder and ventured out for an evening repast. He found a patch of tender aster leaves and began nibbling. Even at a distance I could see the quick-fire motion of his jaws. Without warning he froze upright and stood so still that each strand of fur resisted the breeze. Only the blink of an eye separated the living from the taxidermically prepared. I scanned the area. Coyote? Eagle? Nothing. So eat. And he did, returning to his post a few seconds later. "Marmot behavior has a curiously discontinuous character," a biologist once observed, "like a motion picture that is stopped about every five seconds."

My nervous meadow companion entertained me while a henchman stole into The Renegade and took inventory of the pantry. "Hey! Get the hell out of there!" I yelled. "You little . . . " But nothing was hurt except a bag of freeze-dried chicken. I accepted the loss as the karmic price of my wagering.

My curiosity about marmots gave me an excuse to renew my acquaintance with David Barash, a cheerful man who lives on a ten-acre horse-farm and keeps a Darwin fish tacked like a mezuzah to his door.

Barash gained notoriety following the publication of *The L Word*, his vigorous defense of liberalism written in response to George Bush's derision during the 1988 presidential campaign. Barash was an unrepentant child of the sixties. He'd earned his PhD in zoology at the University of Wisconsin at Madison at the height of that campus's Vietnam War protests. Graduate school memories invoke, he once told me, a cross-modality transfer: "I think of graduate school and I smell tear gas."

Few of his fellow ideologues knew that David Barash, liberal, was also the world's foremost expert on mountain marmots. His interest in marmots grew out of the controversial field of sociobiology. In the 1970s biologists like Edward O. Wilson began developing the idea that social behavior might have a biological basis. That is, a species' way of acting is partly programmed in the genes and changes through evolution and natural selection. Barash, an early believer in sociobiology, wrote the field's introductory textbook. "Ed Wilson for dummies," he calls it.

Marmots give Barash data to test the theory. "There is one genus: *Marmota*," he explained. "And it's widespread throughout the northern hemisphere." There are bobak marmots on the steppes of Kazakhstan, yellow-bellied marmots in the Tetons of Wyoming, Brower's marmots in the Brooks Range of Alaska, Vancouver marmots on Vancouver Island (and nowhere else), Himalayan marmots in Tibet, and woodchucks across the American Northeast. The hoary marmots of Mount Rainier can be found on mountains from the southern Cascades to Alaska and the Northern Rockies. "Structurally, marmots are very much the same, but you have a variety of different species within that genus," said Barash. "Those species are different because they've adapted. What you've got is a controlled evolutionary experiment on a global scale."

The woodchuck exists at one end of the adaptation scale: solitary, intolerant of fellow woodchucks, and sexually prolific. Woodchucks mature at one year and give birth annually. At the other end are the hoaries and the Olympic marmots in the mountains across Puget Sound, who live in social communities, greet each other with cheek-sniffing salutations, and have the slowest reproduction rate of any rodent. "Woodchucks live at the lowest elevation, which means the longest growing season," said Barash. "The hoaries live at the highest elevation, with the shortest growing season. The young grow more slowly at high elevation. The hoaries don't disperse until age two, perhaps because it wouldn't pay the adults to drive away their immature offspring; they would be sabotaging their own genes."

Marmots' high, piercing whistles register a frequency of about 3,000 hertz. (A piano's lowest note resonates at 25 hertz, its highest at 4,000.) Imagine Gracie Allen shrieking, "Eek, a mouse!" only never reaching the *k*. The high pitch may be an evolved defense mechanism. Since it's more difficult to pinpoint the source of a high whistle than that of a modulated voice, a marmot who spots a coyote can sound the hue-and-cry without revealing himself to the predator.

Marmots are a field biologist's dream. They're active only during summer days, they're easy to spot, and they pretty much ignore humans scribbling on clipboards. Mountain goat and elk researchers can spend half their time finding the herd; a marmot researcher who finds a colony won't have to move all summer. Best of all, marmots hibernate from October to May. "They have the convenient habit of being inactive during the academic year," said Barash.

A marmot's front incisors never stop growing, and if it didn't gnaw on rocks and firs they'd jut out like tusks. Adult hoaries lose nearly half their body weight during hibernation and spend all summer putting it back on. They're skinny, furtive, and hungry when they emerge in May, but grow fat and lazy by September. They're exceptionally efficient at producing fat. If humans metabolized food into fat at a similar rate, our butts would be five feet wide. Marmots keep a tight, highly civilized schedule. They eat from about eight until noon, disappear into their burrows for a siesta, then emerge for dinner from five until nine. Then it's time for bed. Each colony constructs a web of underground burrows and overground paths, the location of which they can recall with remarkable precision. "I've seen marmots emerge from hibernation through a couple meters of snow, stand there blinking, and then wander across the snow and excavate the remaining burrow openings— dig straight down, no landmarks," Barash said. Their grass-lined burrows contain distinct sleeping rooms and bathrooms. Safety lies in entrances and exits: A typical colony may have as many as twenty to thirty burrow holes. Once a marmot reaches the burrow, there's no hope of catching it.

A golden eagle can snatch a marmot pup without rustling a blade of grass. As I walked to Mount Fremont one morning, I noticed that the marmots sunning themselves on the talus had suddenly disappeared. I stopped for a sip of water and as I turned to face Burroughs Mountain, a golden eagle the size of a terrier cruised by on a low-level lunch reconnaissance. He worked the winds like a glider, not granting his prey even the warning of a feather cutting through air.

I wonder if humans wouldn't turn into unbearably social beasts if we lived high on the mountain like marmots. Barash's comparison of the independent woodchuck to the communal hoary reminded me of the way environment socializes humans. As a rule, bad weather makes good neighbors. On my block in Seattle, people who usually pass without so much as a glance will greet one another like old friends after a big snowstorm. Any TV news report on a big flood is incomplete without the requisite comment from the mayor about how the crisis "has really brought this town together." The closest neighbors my family ever had were in Alaska, where watching out for each other was the best defense against the common oppression of winter.

Dan Blumstein, a researcher who spent two summers studying the marmots near Sunrise, is fascinated by the marmot's alarm-call altruism. "If there's risk associated with it," he asked, "why take that risk? Is this an example of altruistic behavior?" He isn't convinced the motive is purely unselfish. "Alerting other marmots makes sense in terms of saving your relatives," he said, "saving genes which will ultimately be passed on."

A similar genetic selfishness may underlie our own hard-weather altruism. But I think we're indulging in something more than genetic protection when we pull a neighbor's car out of a snowdrift. When the weather turns against us, our boundaries of "family" widen to embrace our friends, neighbors, and strangers just passing through.

As I left Glacier Basin and continued down the Wonderland Trail, the marmot followed.

MOUNTAIN DREAMS

I walked into Summerland on the last day of summer. On the way up to the camp, I passed signs of the season's leaving. Labor Day campers folded tents, drained coolers, and beat it back to town. One fellow offered me the dregs of his bug juice. "Won't be needing any more of that." Summerland's an easy walk from Glacier Basin, seven miles of mostly shaded woodland or riverside trail, followed by a final mile-long push up switchbacks to a lush subalpine meadow near a tributary of Fryingpan Creek. Above camp the Fryingpan Glacier, a little boutique of ice, sat withered and shrunken in its bed. With no ice to hold its walls together, Little Tahoma—the barb on Rainier's hip—spit rocks onto the Emmons Glacier all day long.

That night winter burst through the door. Rising to heed nature in the predawn dim, I stepped into a brittle world. Frosted fescues shattered under my feet. Dew loogies froze on anemone seedheads and turned the plants into tiny chandeliers. Frost heave cracked the trail and gave emotion to soil. Agony. As if the dirt were moaning from the cold.

It was a mean trick, evicting summer without the notice of autumn. It is the way of the mountain, I told myself, as the latrine welcomed its first morning guest. Feeling smugly at one with nature, I dropped trou and prepared to settle in for a study of the johnny-house wall—*'Phoenix' model backcountry relief station manufactured by Advanced Composting Systems of Whitefish, Montana*—when a shriek issued from my throat the likes of which has never spiraled your cochlea unless you too have cold-sealed your cheeks to the lid.

Winter.

Indian Bar's reputation as a notorious bear enclave can be accounted for by the acres of blueberries surrounding the camp. While they draw the bears, the berries also assure backcountry campers that bears will look upon them as nuisances in the berrypatch rather than two hundred pounds of meat on the hoof. That is, if you arrive during berry season. Which I did not. A ranger had issued me a wilderness permit to pitch my tent among the bears outside the designated camp, but by the time I'd bushwhacked to the top of a ridge above the Ohanapecosh River, I'd begun to question the wisdom of my decision. Every tent-size clearing under every tree bore the wilderness equivalent of a coat on a theater seat: bear scat big as cowpies and puddingly fresh.

Preferring an imperfect bed to the rage of a black bear come home to find me in his crib, I set up camp on an incline steep enough to lift a motorcycle over a fleet of Winnebagos. My tent had never looked thinner, frailer, or more strongly reminiscent of puff pastry.

My evening at Indian Bar was nothing extraordinary. My stove failed, which forced me to eat crunchy freeze-dried "lasagne," and it snowed and the clothes I strung up in the tent froze solid. Another night on the mountain.

I slept fitfully, stumbling between the frightful ambiguity of night sounds and the archfreak world of my dreams. Every time I woke I listened for the sniff of ursa major testing the tenderness of my nylon home. Bears of my mind crept across the meadow. Did I stink? Pit check. Whew! I was broadcasting scent to every sow within a night's trot. In one instant I swear to God I heard a bear, and in the next I told myself it was only snow sliding off the tent. Between two-fifteen and three-fifteen I convinced myself something large and four-legged was lumbering around my campsite. I squatted near the door, my hand grasping the zipper, trying to work up the courage to sneak a peek. In my mind, I saw the creature's breath escape like locomotive smoke from great black nostrils; I heard branches snap under its paws, and small mammals flee for their lives. I worked myself into a paroxysm of fright. I could lie to you and say I banished the night bogie with one quick zip, but the truth is I held the cold zipper in my hand for an hour without finding the guts to open it. Eventually I dropped off to sleep.

I dreamed. Away from the mountain my dreams are ding-dong dull. When friends boast about the surreal clambakes they host during the night, I excuse myself or, if pressed, dredge up that old warhorse in which Tipper Gore and I rescue a planeload of Afghans whose 747 has crashed into a ditch. But alone beneath Rainier's glaciers I became drunk on dreams. At Indian Bar I dreamt myself into a banquet at the Rainier Club, Seattle's Brahman enclave, where heat from floor vents fluttered up runnels of silk drapery and a maze of banquet tables overspilled with roast pork and sauced duck and tumescent sausages strung together like a necklace of bishops. Radiant women glossed the parquet with floor-length gowns. I stood in the middle of it all and—

Then, as they say, I woke up. Cold and hungry, with water dripping on my face.

In *Modern Man in Search of a Soul*, Carl Jung wrote about a colleague who stopped him on the street one day to report "another idiotic dream." In his dream the man climbed a high mountain over steep snow-covered slopes, higher and higher under crystalline skies, until at last he reached the top. "When I reach the summit," the man told Jung, "my happiness and elation are so great that I feel I could mount right up into space." And so he does, climbing right on into thin air and waking in a state of bliss.

Jung, startled by the symbolism of the man's dream, implored him to climb cautiously, if at all, and always with two guides.

"Incorrigible!" said the man, who had always dismissed Jung's dream theories as nonsense.

Two months later a mountain avalanche buried Jung's colleague, but he managed to escape with his life. Three months after that, on an unguided climb, the man stepped into space while descending a peak. "He fell on the head of his friend, who was waiting lower down," wrote Jung, "and both were dashed to pieces far below."

Descartes thought about dreams. Having satisfactorily proven his own existence with the cogito ("I think, therefore et cetera"), he declared himself astonished by man's ability to distinguish the dreaming from the waking state. He solved the dilemma by turning to remembrance. Memory, he wrote, connected the events of our lives as it did not our dreams. Because they had no history, dreams couldn't be real.

One year to the day after beginning my walk around the mountain, it ended—appropriately, in the pouring rain. I woke to two inches of snow above Indian Bar and stayed abed listening to the flakes make soft landings on my tent. Down the ridge the snow turned to slush and sent me skidding rumpwise. For two miles the trail feinted in and out under the quieting white until my altimeter clicked down to 4,900 and the snow turned to rain and the path unwound down through the dim forest. After a year on the mountain, The Renegade felt as comfortable as a cotton shirt and der Wanderschuhe swaddled my feet like glove leather. A survivor's confidence was mine. Striding past Bald Rock and Olallie Creek, watching the trees stretch and fatten as the altitude fell, I felt I could walk all day and into the night. Like Jung's mountaineer I wished I could keep going forever. I'd left behind the trepidation of my first days on the trail; I knew I could survive on the mountain. The fear and fascination I once felt for Rainier had metamorphosed into deeper sentiments. Respect. Regard. Something between affection and love. The experience of walking the mountain had committed Rainier to memory and made it a part of me. Climbers and hikers talk a lot about the thrill of adventure, but I suspect they go into the hills for more than wilderness excitement. Every day spent on Rainier strengthens the bond between the landscape and our own identity; we create a personal history that gives meaning to the mountain. We know people by their stories: their history, their habits, their secrets, their triumphs and failures. We know them by what they *do*. We want to know mountains, too, but they've got no story. So we do the next best thing. We throw ourselves onto them and make the stories happen. By casting ourselves onto Rainier's dangerous flanks, we make the mountain our own. My own history with the mountain remained incomplete. I'd wandered about its lower elevations—to 7,000 feet, less than halfway up—but had yet to see what lay up high. I began to crave the stories that might come in the upper reaches. As I carried my soggy load off the mountain, I remembered the name of a mountain climber a friend had told me about. I'd go see him, I decided, and ask what it was all about.

My father met me at Ohanapecosh and we drove into town and ordered steak, rare, and I told him my story.

FISCHER

D*ead.*"

Scott Fischer slapped a slide of the British climber Alison Hargreaves on the table.

"Dead." A shot of Canadian climber Jeff Lakes.

"Dead." New Zealander Bruce Grant.

On a rainy Tuesday night in Seattle, Fischer and his friend Peter Goldman huddled over a pile of Kodachromes in the office of Fischer's guide service, Mountain Madness. As they sorted the carousels of their recent trip to Pakistan's Karakoram Range, Fischer's voice rose in anger as the gallery of fallen climbers passed through his fingers.

"Who are these?" Goldman asked, holding a frame to the light.

"Dead."

Scott Fischer was a tall, tightly muscled mountain guide who bound his flaxen hair in a horsetail that swished across his upper back. Premature wrinkles creeked into his forty-year-old eyes because he had spent his life closer to the sun than the rest of us. He had climbed Everest and he had climbed K2. In 1995 he led Goldman and six others on a two-month climb to Broad Peak, K2's next-door neighbor.

Along the way Fischer's expedition met climbers going to K2, including Hargreaves, one of England's most famous adventurers. They shared a base camp, food, and the tentbound days that are the price of any high mountain trip. They befriended Hargreaves and other K2 climbers: Lakes, Grant, the American Rob Slater, and three Spaniards, Javier Ecartin, Javier Olivar, and Lorenzo Ortiz. Fischer snapped portraits to pass the time. A month later and half a world away, those slides were all he had left. Because on the morning Fischer and his team summited Broad Peak, one of K2's notorious storms battered Hargreaves and the others. While Fischer and Goldman relaxed with bottles of Bridgeport Ale in Seattle, the K2 team was—

"Dead."

I'd gone to ask Fischer why he climbed the biggest mountains in the world, an activity that seemed to me utterly indefensible. Climbing to the top of the world required more than curiosity and will; it also demanded an abundance of ego and hubris. The high mountains remain one of the Earth's few spots where humanity is denied access, and this doesn't strike me as a too-restrictive barrier. Why shouldn't there be places we can't reach? What was up there, anyway?

With Fischer I got more than I bargained for. His life became an argument both for and against climbing. In one year he was involved in two of the worst climbing accidents in contemporary mountaineering history. He told me why he climbed. And then he climbed. And then he died.

On the night I met him he was still alive and recovering from the Karakoram trip and the deaths of his colleagues. Peter Goldman picked up a slide.

"Whoa," said Goldman. "Is this Lakes? Which one is Jeff Lakes?"

"He's the one who fuckin' crawled down and died, man."

Jeff Lakes turned back early on the K2 summit day, only to be swept up in an avalanche. He dug himself out and spent the night without a sleeping bag at 26,000 feet. The next morning he crawled down thousands of feet without crampons or an ice axe, which is to a climber as a brake pedal is to a driver. When he reached a lower camp, barely alive, Lakes's friends filled him with warm liquids and wrapped him in a sleeping bag. He fell asleep and never woke up.

Fischer passed a slide to Goldman. "Remember him? Slater?"

"Never forget him. Who's this?"

"Bruce Grant. Here's another one of Slater."

"Jesus Christ. You should send some to Slater's family."

"Already did."

The first rule of mountain climbing: Nothing counts if you don't make it down. "K2 doesn't appear on those people's climbing résumés," Fischer told me, "because their résumés are done." George Mallory, the British explorer who answered "Because it is there" when asked why he wanted to climb Mount Everest, established the principle in 1924. Mallory may have walked over the hump of Everest that year and died on the way down. Nobody knows. His body was never found.

His triumph didn't count. In 1953 Edmund Hillary and Tenzing Norgay made it down. Theirs counted.

When mountaineers mention climbing résumés, they aren't speaking metaphorically. Applying for a spot on a Himalayan expedition often involves faxing a tally of ascents to the expedition leader. It's like landing a job or getting into college. Scott Fischer's résumé included unaided summits of Everest and K2. (The air is so thin on the high peaks that most climbers breathe from oxygen tanks. Climbing "unaided" without supplemental oxygen increases a climber's fatigue and reduces the chance of success.) He had led climbs up Alaska's Mount McKinley, Africa's Kilimanjaro, South America's Aconcagua, and Asia's Mount Communism, Ama Dablam, and Baruntse. He had stood on the highest points of six continents. There may have been nobody in the world better at getting people up and back down the world's deadliest mountains. Physical strength accounted for only part of Fischer's success; more important was his attitude, a mixture of Zen calm and balls-for-the-summit tenacity. And, he would remind you, the ability to make the right choices.

As Fischer sorted his Karakoram slides, the phone rang with congratulations and queries about his upcoming Everest expedition. Between calls he sipped his beer and mulled over the theory of choices, which went something like this: You make the right ones, you live; you make the wrong ones, you die. Alison Hargreaves made the wrong ones.

"We summited on Broad Peak about ten in the morning and were back in our high camp when the storm blew in," he said. "We were pulling into camp about the time they were summiting—six at night. There was an outrageous wind whipping up a ground blizzard, it's blowing old snow in your face, it's painful. We're working hard just to keep our tents up. The people on K2 are exposed and a mile higher. I can't imagine what it was like for them."

Every climber has a set of Stay Alive rules. Fischer's most important was the Two O'Clock Rule. If you hadn't made it up top by two, it was time to turn around. Darkness was not your friend. The K2 climbers wanted the summit so badly they ignored the rule. "They summited at six-thirty that night," Fischer said. "Six-thirty! Did they think someone was going to turn on the lights when they wanted to go back down? That's being harsh, but . . . " His voice trailed off, leaving his listener to fill in the blank: " . . . but seven people died."

I walked away from Fischer's office that night exhilarated and disgusted. Welcome to the world of mountain climbing, where the stakes are elusive glory and death.

The climbing world has its own specialists: rock climbers, ice climbers, and big-mountain climbers. There are so few big-mountain experts that they could probably all fit in one room. There are reasons for this. First, it costs. The budget for an Everest expedition can approach one million dollars. (A two-day guided Rainier climb costs around four hundred fifty dollars per person, not including equipment.) The countries that border the big peaks—Nepal, Pakistan, India, China—don't make it easy to obtain climbing permits. Fischer retained a consultant in Kathmandu to guide his applications through the Third World bureaucracy. And, of course, people die. For every three climbers who make it to the top of Mount Everest, one dies trying. A big-mountain climber who hasn't lost a friend hasn't been climbing long.

Fischer was among the handful of Pacific Northwesterners who attained full membership in the big-mountain club. In the 1960s an earlier generation of local climbers pioneered routes up the Himalayas and became American climbing icons: Jim Whittaker, who became the first American atop Everest in 1963; the late climber-philosopher Willi Unsoeld; Spokane mountaineer John Roskelley; Seattle attorney Jim Wickwire. In the 1990s, membership remains highly exclusive. Local initiates include Ed Viesturs, who has climbed nine of the fourteen mountains that rise more than 8,000 meters (about 26,250 feet) above the sea; Greg Child, author of *Thin Air: Encounters in the Himalayas*; Steve Swenson, who climbed Everest and K2; Todd Burleson, a veteran of eight Everest expeditions; and Scott Fischer.

Fischer was a guide's guide who possessed the sort of rugged handsomeness and assured grace that made women want to be with him and men want to be him. He loved nothing more than getting other people to the tops of high mountains. His climbing partners proclaimed him a master at "grooving" on mountains. "If you ain't grooving, you're bumming," he'd say, "and grooving's a lot funner, so let's groove on up this mountain." He was not everybody's chum. The leaders of the 1988 Everest expedition, on which Stacy Allison became the first American woman to reach the summit, rejected Fischer after his in-person interview. He had a natural confidence that was easy to interpret as cockiness, and maybe it was. A year after his Broad Peak trip, Fischer planned to climb Gasherbrum IV, a terrifying Karakoram pinnacle about ten miles south of K2. Steve Swenson, who had turned back on three previous Gasherbrum attempts, had asked him to come along.

"When Steve asked me to climb Gasherbrum with him, I told him no," Fischer said. "Not interested. Don't want to go, spend two to three months on Gasherbrum and fail. He says, 'Well, I'm gonna climb to the top of it.' You tried three times already, I said, what's the deal? And he had the perfect answer. Said, 'If I'd been with you, we'd a-gotten there.'"

Wes Krause, Fischer's early guide-service partner, once told the story of a climb with Fischer in Alaska's Wrangell Range. There had been recent reports of grizzly sightings near the climbing trail, and the two got to talking about what to do if they happened upon a hungry ursa.

"Aw hell, if he charges we'll just take him on with our ice axes," Fischer joked.

A few hours later the climbers spotted a grizzly, the grizzly spotted them, and the former charged the latter. Krause dropped his pack and ran. "I turned to look back, and there's Fischer standing there pulling his ice axe out of his pack."

If you wanted to get up Everest in the 1960s or 1970s, you had to earn your climbing stripes and wait for a call from one of the Whittaker brothers, or whoever was planning the trip, to invite you aboard. Nowadays it's more straightforward. If you've got high-altitude experience and sixty-five thousand dollars, there are a number of guides who will get you to base camp. You still need a little experience on your résumé; nobody's going to give you an ice axe lesson on Everest's Khumbu Icefall. And you still have to climb the mountain on your own two legs.

Everest's new accessibility rankles some climbers because it threatens to turn one of the world's great challenges into a packaged tourist trip.

It also changes the dynamic on the mountain, from one in which everyone is an assumed expert to one in which less-experienced clients follow a guide up the hill. "A lot of serious climbers think it's a shame that Everest has been devalued," writer and climber Jon Krakauer told me. "They think it's become a trophy for rich, over-achieving stockbrokers."

Other climbers are all for it. "Some of the older climbers aren't happy about it, but I think it's great," said Brent Bishop, an accomplished climber and son of Barry Bishop, who documented the 1963 American expedition for *National Geographic*. "It brings money to the climbing community, to guides, Sherpas, and the [Nepalese] economy. If someone has that kind of money, I'm for climbing Everest instead of sitting on your ass drinking martinis at the country club."

Everest's popularity has turned it into an experiment in mountain management. More than five hundred people have reached the summit, most within the last ten years. By the early 1990s the mountain had become so crowded that one day in 1993, forty climbers jostled elbows on the summit. Embarrassed by traffic jams at the summit and piles of trash at base camp, the Nepalese government raised the permit fee from ten thousand dollars per expedition to ten thousand dollars per climber, limited the number of teams, and required a four-thousand-dollar equipment deposit to make sure those who packed in oxygen tanks also packed them out. In 1994 Brent Bishop led a team, with Fischer as the climbing leader, on a garbage run to the top of the world. They hauled away more than five thousand pounds of junk, including two hundred oxygen tanks.

The overcrowding of Everest doesn't augur well for Rainier. The growing popularity of mountain climbing among the well-heeled is likely to trickle down to the middle class, for whom Rainier stands as an enticing challenge. That the mountain hasn't already been overrun by sport climbers is largely due to the fact that since 1968 only Rainier Mountaineering Incorporated (RMI) has been allowed to operate within the national park. (About one-third of all Rainier climbers use RMI; the rest climb in self-guided parties.) The single-service policy has preserved the mountain but kept guides like Scott Fischer from working in their own backyard.

Most RMI expeditions use the popular Disappointment Cleaver route that runs through Camp Muir, but a few five-day seminars go up the Emmons Glacier on the mountain's eastern flank. In recent years park officials have considered giving a second guide service exclusive rights to the Emmons route, but they don't know if the mountain can handle the impact of a second service. "Every physical resource has a limit of some sort," said Glenn Baker, who oversaw Rainier's guide concession for the National Park Service in the early 1990s. "When you overcrowd that resource, you detract from the qualities that made it worthy of being a national park in the first place. At what point do you say, 'Hold off—no more'? We don't know. We don't have the funds to research these things, so the best we can do is [make] an educated guess." (In April 1997, the Park Service awarded the Emmons route to Cascade Alpine Guides, one of Fischer's competitors.)

The problem isn't limited to Rainier. In recent years Yosemite National Park officials have closed the park's gates when holiday crowds have overrun the grounds. In a culture increasingly disconnected from the natural world, our national parks have become wilderness repositories. Instead of tending the remnants of the prepavement world that exist around us, we pack up for the weekend and visit mountains and monuments where the glaciers, rivers, and forests are kept as in a zoo. As the world's population expands, the mountains are bound to be either overrun or held in trust by state officials who peddle access to the highest bidders. "There is a growing population base that has money," Fischer told me. "There is a finite amount of wilderness. There are going to be more and more people every year who want to climb Mount Rainier. That's just a fact. And there's only one Mount Rainier."

Scott Fischer let his life stand as his best argument for climbing. Leading other people up mountains allowed him to live a perpetual adventure. Between his late summer return from Broad Peak and his spring departure for Everest, he flew to Kathmandu to secure Everest permits, visited Denmark to drum up publicity for a Danish climber on his Everest team, taught an ice climbing seminar in Colorado, led a charity fundraising climb up Mount Kilimanjaro, trained for Everest, and flew again to Kathmandu.

I asked Fischer why he worked like this, hanging out in some of the world's most dangerous places. "They're the most beautiful places in the world," he said. "I like hanging out at base camp. There's no phone or fax. Your life is very, very simple. You're playing a survival game. Your decisions have consequence."

But why take the risk? I asked. What do you find on the summit?

"It's business," he answered. "This is something I'm good at. It's what I do. And there's a demand for it.

"The summit experience is valuable because not many people in the world can have it. I don't go for the view. Seems like every time I get to a mountaintop, there's no view. I do it for the accomplishment, for the lifestyle, for the travel. There's *nobody* that can say it's fun. When I get to the top of a mountain, I'm immediately figuring how long I can be there before I go back down."

I pressed, trying to coax from him some deeper reflection on the mysticism and meaning of mountains. But for Fischer the meaning of mountains lay in their lack of complexity; up high the world's extraneous parts simply fell away. That was as deep as it got with him. If you wanted more you'd have to climb the mountain yourself.

After four Everest expeditions Fischer believed he'd learned what worked and what didn't. Weather, for instance. Every year around the tenth of May, a high pressure ridge moves in over Everest, providing a few days of clear weather. "I used to think: May tenth will be the summit day, but boy, I'm going to be ready on April twenty-fifth, hanging out at a high camp, and when the weather's nice I'm going to go." He smiles and cocks his head in a way that indicates, *I found out that was stupid*. "Can't do that. Look, the highest civilization anywhere in the world is fifteen, sixteen thousand feet high. If you spend weeks carrying heavy loads up to a high camp, if you go on living at twenty-four thousand feet for days on end, you're up there thinking, *It's gonna happen soon*. But the only thing that's happening is your body is going downhill." Fischer's new plan was to sink fixed ropes (safety lines anchored in the snow) from base to the higher camps, then let his body rest at lower altitude. By the time his clients arrived in April, he planned to have the route all but fixed by his Sherpa team.

Fischer's Sherpas were led by Lobsang Jangbu, a twenty-three-year-old Nepalese climber possessed of smoldering good looks, a gold tooth, and Everest experience that included two summits without oxygen.

"Let me tell you a Lobsang story," Fischer said. "When we climbed Everest in 1994, there were probably twenty people trying to get up along the South Col on the same day." (The popular South Col route was taken by Edmund Hillary and Jim Whittaker on their respective climbs. Veterans refer to it as the milk run.) "Everybody knows everybody else, we're all sharing a base camp. Lobsang, Rob Hess, and myself were the only ones going up without oxygen. Everyone's telling us we gotta leave early, that they'll pass us on the way, make sure we're doing okay. We took off about one-thirty in the morning, ahead of everybody else. Never saw them the whole way up. Got to the top in about nine and a half hours. When we get up there, Lobsang starts unloading his pack. He takes out this big foam cowboy hat and puts it on, wants us to take his picture. Then he reaches into the pack and pulls out two oxygen tanks that he'd brought along the whole way— just in case Rob or I ran into trouble."

The last time I spoke with him, Fischer was fixing last-minute Everest logistical glitches and training at night in a Seattle climbing gym. He was excited about his Everest team, which included Neal Beidleman, an Aspen mountaineer who had accompanied Fischer to K2 a few years earlier; Lene Gammelgaard, who aspired to become the first Danish woman on Everest; Sandy Hill Pittman, a Manhattan socialite in pursuit of the highest summits on the seven continents; Anatoli Boukreev, a Russian guide and former coach of Kazakhstan's national cross-country ski team; and Pete Schoening, a sixty-seven-year-old mountaineer whose legendary ice axe arrest had saved the lives of his entire rope team on the 1953 American K2 expedition. Schoening was bringing his nephew Klev along. "That's a two-pack, as we say in the business," Fischer said.

"It's a very strong team," he told me. Summiting Everest would complete the elder Schoening's own Seven Summits bid. Sandy Pittman was attempting the mountain again after falling short on two earlier expeditions. "This time she's going with the right guy," he said.

A few days earlier the BBC had broadcast a report on the journey Alison Hargreaves's husband and two children had taken to Pakistan to see the mountain where she died. The audiotape was heartbreaking. "Is Mummy up there?" one of the children asked through a stream of tears. I asked Fischer, the father of an eight-year-old son and a four-year-old daughter, how he and his wife Jeannie dealt with the risk he took every time he went into the mountains. He didn't hesitate.

"I believe one hundred percent I'm coming back, so it's not difficult for me. My wife believes one hundred percent I'm coming back. She isn't concerned about me when I'm guiding, because I'm gonna make all the right choices.

"When accidents happen, I think it's always human error. That's what I want to eliminate. I've had lots of climbing accidents in my youth. You come up with lots of reasons, but ultimately it's human error: You made a choice to put yourself in that spot. Even avalanches. Avalanches are predictable. That doesn't mean I'm not gonna cross an avalanche field, but it should be a conscious choice. The key factor is choosing what I'm gonna climb.

"I don't climb to get scared," he said. "I climb not to be scared."

Scott Fischer didn't come back. On May 10, 1996, summit day, Fischer's Mountain Madness business partner Karen Dickinson called to tell me they'd just heard from base camp. Fischer's team had summited ten climbers, a spectacular success. Fischer, Boukreev, Beidleman, and Jangbu had led six clients—including Pittman, Gammelgaard, and Klev

Schoening—to the top. At the Mountain Madness office, Dickinson broke out the champagne.

The next day Dickinson's husband, Paul Roberts, who is an old friend, left a message on my answering machine. "Bruce . . . ahh . . . just wanted to let you know that they haven't been able to find Mr. Fischer on Everest. He didn't make it back to camp and . . . may not."

I called Paul at the Mountain Madness office and he told me it didn't look good. Scott had been gone too long.

Not knowing what to do, I sat in my apartment and played Paul's message again. " . . . just wanted to let you know . . . find Mr. Fischer . . . may not." The oddment of "Mr." connected to Fischer's name struck me as awkward and chilling, like a code word conveying a message that there's trouble at the other end of the line. The strained formality also seemed the first yard of distance opening up between the living and the dead.

That night I considered driving into the mountains. But before I could lace up my boots, I was struck with the realization that mountains were the last place I wanted to be. I'd had enough of the goddamn mountains and Scott Fischer's simple choices. Where I wanted to be was smack in the middle of the most abmountainal environment imaginable. Which is why I slipped into a pair of slacks and walked to the Seattle Center Opera House, where Umberto Giordano's *Andrea Chenier* was concluding a two-week run. Before curtain time, my eyes roved about the audience, delighting in the women who tilted their heads to let the houselights dance in the diamonds pinned to their ears, and admiring the bravado of men who wore bow ties and vests streaked with gold thread. The overheads dimmed, the murmur hushed, and the curtain rose on the opening scene, in which the young poet Chenier is introduced at an aristocratic gala in France, *avant la révolution*. The colors! The warmth, the laughter, the rich baritone of the leading man's voice!

Thirty rows from the stage, I swirled in a dissonant whirl. I couldn't stop thinking about Fischer freezing to death in a cold and silent world, and I couldn't stop reveling in the creamy pleasures around me. The chandeliers! The drapery! The powdered wigs! The ladies lost in fountains of panniers, ruffles, and lace. The scents of Chanel and Dior floating through the hall. The upswept coif of the woman in front of me that was about to collapse because of an ill-considered placement of a hairpin. It was all I could do to keep from crying. I luxuriated in the sensual overwhelm of it all, feeling magnificently alive and as full of the wonder of the civilized world as a man tucked into a featherbed while the king of France pours velvet down his throat.

For the next week those who knew him kept their ears cocked to the radio, expecting to hear news of Fischer's spectacular descent, about how he'd walked down Everest on frozen legs while the rest of the world counted him dead and gone. But sometimes the world counts correctly.

Summit day occurred on the date he'd predicted—May 10, 1996— but Fischer broke his cardinal rule and summited too late. Lobsang Jangbu failed to install the crucial fixed ropes up high, electing instead to short-rope Sandy Pittman to the summit. (Short-roping is when a guide clips a client to a short rope and pulls him or her up the mountain. Some guides call it "water skiing.") Fischer pulled in at the tail end of a train of climbers and was the last to reach the summit, at three-thirty that afternoon. A sudden storm hit the mountain, pummeling those up top. Though he used supplemental oxygen, Fischer's legendary strength failed him on the way down, and so did his mind. According to one report, Jangbu short-roped Fischer's descent as long as he could, then stayed with his friend until he had to leave for his own safety. Fischer told his climbing partner he wanted to jump down to camp.

Late the next evening Anatoli Boukreev found Fischer's remains on the path above the South Col, his mittens off and his jacket open. The Russian removed his friend's body from the trail and lashed it to the mountain with rope. When you die on a high mountain, that is where you stay. Surviving climbers barely have the strength to lower themselves down, let alone carry a two-hundred-pound corpse.

Ten other climbers died in the storm, including Rob Hall, the veteran Everest guide who was on his eighth expedition to the top of the world. All of Fischer's guides and clients survived except him.

A few days after Fischer's death I visited Jane Bromet, a climber who had first put me in touch with Fischer. She'd trekked in to Mountain Madness's Everest base camp a few weeks earlier and returned with a videotape of the trip. I watched the tape as she answered phone calls from friends and reporters.

In one scene Fischer and Neal Beidleman took advantage of a rest stop along a Himalayan trail to tick off the legendary peaks around them. "We're trekking up to Everest base camp," Beidleman said into the camera. "We're at about 14,400 feet right now. It's a gorgeous day, could be in shorts. Kinda chilly just sitting here." Wind hisses in the background. "Over there you can see Lhotse, the fourth highest peak in the world—"

"I climbed that!" Fischer broke in, laughing.

"—just barely see the top of Everest, which Scott has also climbed. Makalu, the fifth highest peak—"

"Neal climbed that!"

"And Baruntse—"

"We do have a smattering of a Baruntse view over there—I climbed that!"

"They've all been done," said Beidleman. "There's nothing left. We're gonna go up to Everest anyway. Because I haven't climbed that. Gonna have some fun."

Lou Whittaker, who has lost many friends in the mountains, once wrote that he can't abide people who say, "At least he or she died doing something they loved."

"No way!" Whittaker wrote. "You don't want to die in the mountains. You want to live so you can enjoy the mountains another day."

Scott Fischer knew what he was doing. He didn't want to die in the mountains. "I've seen a lot of death in the past three years," he said before leaving for Everest. "I've been close myself. It's a really, really dangerous sport. But I have no regrets. That's the game you're choosing to play. These are very successful, very driven, very fun-loving adventurous people. These are the best people in the world. These are my friends."

One of the last scenes in Bromet's video showed Fischer clipping his backpack in place, checking his crampons, adjusting his visor, then waving and turning into the Khumbu Icefall, the first big hurdle to the top. The sun flared off the freeze, which looked slick as ice cubes left on the counter. Fischer walked off and up with no sound but the soft wind. And then a voice that he didn't hear.

"'Bye, Scott."

CLIFFHANGERS

Fischer in death left me with more questions than he'd answered in life. "He did what he loved," other climbers told me. "He was driven; he had to climb." Oh, come on, I thought. There had to be more to it than climbing-bum slogans. It seemed incomprehensible that anyone would leave wife and family for months at a time in order to live on the Earth's barren seams. It seemed especially cruel to die so far from home. My search for answers sent me to my climbing books. I've always tried to understand the world through the written word. Perhaps, I thought, some mountain memoirs would contain reflections on making the choice to go high. Perhaps they'd tell me why.

I began with *Accidents in North American Mountaineering*, a record of all the avalanches, rockfalls, lightning strikes, crevasse plunges, and thousand-foot ice tumbles that kill, on average, thirty North American climbers each year. This is the climbing story in the raw—nothing but exquisitely detailed calamity—and for real-life harrowism its volumes are hard to beat. Fred Beckey, the legendary Northwestern climber, slips through his harness as a friend adjusts a strap: "Beckey grabbed [his partner's] pack, only to find that it was all he held. A few seconds later a thud was heard below." Another fellow vanishes on Mount St. Helens, "last seen skiing down the east side of the Dog's Head." Bounding rock crushes one alpinist's skull. Another suffers grand mal seizures on Mount McKinley. Every few years some hapless climber sticks himself with his own ice axe—in the ear, forearm, leg, or worse. "In falling," one report reads, "the shaft of his ice axe pierced his scrotum."

I moved on to fuller narratives and watched the body count rise. In Peter Boardman and Joe Tasker's *Boardman Tasker Omnibus*, Reinhold Messner's *Free Spirit*, Joe Simpson's *This Game of Ghosts*, Jon Krakauer's *Eiger Dreams*, frozen stiffs rain like bankers in a market crash. Departed colleagues are reduced to asides: "After Dougal Haston's death in an avalanche . . . "; "I read that Rob Uttley was gone, dying alone on his first Himalayan expedition . . . " Kills on some mountains are recorded like stencils on a warplane's fuselage. All you need to know about the North Face of the Eiger, the most feared peak in the Alps, is that an Italian climber who died there hung from his rope, "unreachable but visible to the curious below for three years," writes Jon Krakauer, "alternately sealed into the ice sheath of the wall and swaying in the winds of summer."

For all the trauma, mountaineers are astonishingly casual about death. Photographs of fellow climbers are labeled "before he was killed in the Verdon Gorge" or "before they died . . . near Kathmandu." The longer you linger in this library of death, the more natural the captions seem. Erasure from the list of the quick confers glory all 'round: on the dead for proving their will to climb, on the mountain for the new respect it demands, and on the survivors for their courage to continue in the face of disaster. Unlike any other sport, mountaineering demands that its players die.

Mountain climbing is the most literary of all sports. Baseball inspires more grandstand elegists, but no other activity so compels its participants to turn each private conquest into a public tale. A mountain climb is a ready-made narrative, perfectly suited to story. The characters gather beneath the great rock and encounter increasingly perilous situations on their way up. Some may die. In the end they snatch glory on the summit or turn back humbled by the brutal force of nature. End of story.

The mountaineering tale is a distant relation of the exploration narrative, that once-grand house of literature that includes Richard Hakluyt's sixteenth-century voyage collections, William Dampier's South Seas adventures, James Cook's Pacific travels, Lewis and Clark's westward journey, and Ernest Shackleton's polar odyssey. Where the classic exploration book sprang from the dry prose of a captain's log, the climbing narrative is rooted in verse. Many early climbers were poets who tramped through the Alps in search of the sublime. The eighteenth-century English poet Thomas Gray found the high peaks savage, horrid places that yielded "the most poetical scenes imaginable . . . You have Death perpetually before your eyes," he wrote.

Sport climbers displaced the poets in the late eighteenth century, turning out books that were part Baedeker, part *Adventure Stories for Boys*. Horace Bénédict de Saussure's *Voyages dans les Alpes,* an account of his trips into the Swiss Alps, introduced English and European tourists to the mountains in 1779. De Saussure, a wealthy Genevan, is generally acknowledged as the first recreational mountaineer. In his climbing history *Ascent*, Jeremy Bernstein notes that de Saussure recorded an ascent of Mont Blanc on which he was accompanied by one servant and eighteen guides who portered mattresses, bed linen, two green jackets, a white suit and three vests, five pairs of shoes, silk and wool stockings, six half-bottles of white wine, two half-bottles of eau de cerises, and a parasol up the high mountain cliffs.

A century after de Saussure, Edward Whymper's popular 1871 travelogue *Scrambles Amongst the Alps* set the form for all subsequent mountaineering pulps: Recount the climb in crag-by-crevice detail and play the peril for all it's worth. "This, it must be understood, was a situation where not only might a slip have been fatal to every one, but it would have been so beyond doubt," writes Whymper in mid-ascent; "nothing, moreover, was easier than to make one."

Those early climbers were true explorers; their authors recorded the first descriptions of uncharted peaks. When the Alps ran out of virgin rock, the mountaineers went to Alaska, the Himalayas, the Andes. In the 1920s the world's top climbers turned their attention to unconquered Asian summits, especially Everest. Publishers cleverly masked the failure of each expedition with titles like *Mount Everest: The Reconnaissance, 1921; The Assault on Mount Everest, 1922;* and *The Fight for Everest, 1924.* By the late 1930s the datemark had been abandoned in favor of a safer titling policy. Thus, *Everest: The Unfinished Adventure.*

For thirty years Everest stood undefeated, one of the Earth's final terrestrial challenges. When Edmund Hillary and Tenzing Norgay broke the spell in 1953, they inspired a new generation of mountaineers and sparked great public interest in Himalayan adventure. John Hunt's *The Ascent of Everest*, Wilfrid Noyce's *South Col*, Kenneth Mason's *Abode of Snow*, Hillary's *High Adventure*, and Ralph Izzard's *An Innocent on Everest* were knocked out within a year of the historic conquest. Reading about these authors' innocent curiosity about the world's high places makes one recall a time not so long ago when the Earth still held secrets.

Hillary and Norgay became world-renowned mountaineering icons, but they also brought climbing's age of discovery to a close. The moment the lanky New Zealander and his Sherpa partner stepped up to 29,028 feet, every mountain explorer turned into a common sportsman. The early Everest books were driven by the climb; now the climbs tend to be driven by the books. Sandy Hill Pittman left for Everest on Scott Fischer's expedition with a publisher's contract in hand and an NBC-sponsored World Wide Web page ready to pixelcast her diary to the electronic world. Pittman survived; her book will undoubtedly sell well. Other climbers aren't so lucky. In 1985 a heavily indebted British climber decided the fastest route to fiscal health led up Everest's North Face. Royalties from his story, he figured, would quiet the creditor's knock. His scheme worked. He died.

By the 1970s most of the world's major peaks had been scaled. In the 1980s base camps became base villages, with encampments of American, British, Japanese, French, German, Italian, and Czech climbers floating a cutthroat trade in Gaz canisters and driving one another batty with boom boxes. Desperate to wring some new challenge out of the hills, climbers turned to fine-print *Guinness Book* stunts: first solo one-day climb of Everest, first live video from Everest, first paraglider flight from Everest. With each achievement the stakes grew higher; among top mountaineers the challenge now isn't to climb one 8,000-meter peak but to summit all fourteen. The fresh mountain air has staled; it carries the tang of *fin de siècle* boredom and desperation. Peter Boardman sums up the problem: "There's a shortage of blanks on maps."

While mountain climbers invented ever more technical "firsts," mountain writers turned in the only direction left: inside. So many ascents have been documented, writes Boardman in *The Shining Mountain,* that "only the mountaineer's inner self remains the uncharted." The climbing memoir seems particularly well suited to egobiography, that self-help tale wherein the hero, through luck, pluck, and a good therapist, finds happiness in self-acceptance. This affinity has been exploited most readily by Stacy Allison, the first American woman to reach the summit of Mount Everest. Her book, *Beyond the Limits: A Woman's Triumph on Everest,* could be subtitled "The Story of My Self-Esteem." The great British mountaineer George Mallory climbed Everest, famously, "because it is there"; Stacy Allison climbs it because her self-confidence is not. After breaking up with an abusive husband, she convinces herself that reaching the top of the world's highest peak "would cleanse my spirit and heal my wounds." Climbing Everest would not only repair her personal life, it would affix the First American Woman title to her name and shield her against the spears of self-doubt. On the mountain, however, her dreams unravel. She finds herself competing against Mimi, another woman on the expedition.

Both covet the First American Woman honor, but "I needed it more," Allison writes. "Mimi already had all the self-esteem in the world."

Days stretch into weeks and months with nothing to do but stare at tent walls and nurse resentments. Camp society regresses to the level of the school playground, and Allison's narrative slips into the tone of an adolescent diary. "Mimi's nastiness made me mad," she reports. "It's one thing to have doubts about your climbing partners. Making them so clear to everyone in such a public way seemed gratuitously mean." Allison's quest for self-esteem becomes so overbearing that I couldn't help rooting for Nasty Mimi's triumphant return. Alas, no. In the end Allison claims her title and the winner's share of self-esteem. "The real triumph comes when you can accept yourself in any weather and in any state," she announces, "and still be able to say: That's me, and I'm okay." I put down the book and wondered: For this you needed to climb Everest?

The other favorite theme of contemporary climbers is the saga of self-inflicted suffering endured against impossible odds for no rational purpose. As a primer in self-sought agony, it would be hard to surpass the massive *Boardman Tasker Omnibus*. British mountaineers Peter Boardman and Joe Tasker became two of climbing's brightest stars in the late seventies and early eighties by scaling unforgiving Asian peaks like Changabang, K2, Kangchenjunga, and Everest, then recounting the adventure in volumes like *Savage Arena* (Tasker) and *Sacred Summits* (Boardman). The stories, collected in the *Omnibus*, are as patterned as a Butterick dress: The intended climb must be suicidal. Friends will wax skeptical. Loved ones will beg, "For God's sake, don't go!" "Just the two of you?" a colleague says of their plan to scale the Himalayan peak Changabang. "Sounds like cruelty to me." Yet our men have no choice. They must go, and go the hard way, dismissing the ascent line of a previous expedition as a "married man's route." (Climbers' personal relationships tend to fall apart when they're not bound by perlon line. The dumping of a climber by his or her spouse is so common that it's almost a pre-expedition ritual. I claim no immunity from the problem.)

Once an author is on the mountain, there's no limit to what he'll suffer for his reader. "I . . . clawed the rock with senseless, bleeding fingers," writes Tasker. "It was so cold that each piton, each karabiner stuck to my hand and took away a little more skin." Lose a few digits to the cause? All the better. Reinhold Messner's *Free Spirit* features a photograph of the author's frostbite-blackened feet taken just after a retreat from the Kashmiri peak Nanga Parbat and just before the author became Reinhold the Four-Toed. Lou Whittaker, Mount Rainier's jovial elder statesman, knows what it's like to have both eyeballs freeze on Mount Everest. It hurts. And yet, he writes in *Memoirs of a Mountain Guide*, it's not the worst thing. The worst thing is feeling them thaw. "The pain was unbelievable," writes Whittaker, "the worst I have ever experienced."

The toil and suffering that in Edmund Hillary's day were means to the end of mountain exploration have now become ends in themselves. The challenge is to see how much punishment the body can withstand. And in this competition, even Frozen-Eyed Lou must yield to agony's champion, a mountaineer named Joe Simpson, whose wit seems as dim as his body is resilient. "I wanted a 'tick list' of hard routes under my belt," he writes in *This Game of Ghosts*. "I wanted to be a great climber." Instead, he slips down ropes. He swims through avalanches. He camps beneath rockfalls. He sets his tent on fire. He tosses a boot on a 13,000-foot ridge. In *This Game of Ghosts* the climbing tale reaches its contemporary apogee. If Joe Simpson were running diphtheria serum to Nome, his survival might provide some measure of satisfaction, even uplift, to the reader. Instead we're faced with the three-hundred-thirty-page story of a man addicted to thrill. I found the experience titillating but small.

Climbers are occasionally troubled by their unjustifiable acts. They are, after all, seeking out environments of hardship where none exists naturally in their lives. A tentbound day spent reading Zola's *Germinal* induces an episode of guilt in Peter Boardman. "Unlike the miners in France . . . struggling for daily survival against harsh physical conditions," he writes, "[Tasker] and I were here seeking a survival situation . . . Our adventure was a pampered luxury that we could afford to enjoy, it was pure self-indulgence." Boardman is a veritable Socrates compared to his colleagues. When Reinhold Messner returns to Nanga Parbat a year after his first disastrous trip, the mountain villagers are eager for him to answer the question they'd been mulling over all winter: "Why had I had to go over the mountain and not around it in order to get from one valley to the other?" Messner offers no answer. Nor does he seem particularly intrigued by the question. After a lively conversation in sign language and broken Urdu, the author peels off his socks for a toes-and-stumps display. "The peasants contemplated me with shaking heads." I joined them.

I closed my books not with a heightened respect for the high peaks and the people who climb them, but with a peculiar kind of sadness. The ever more extreme lengths to which Messner et al. must go to challenge the mountains only drive home the realization that in the postindustrial world, nature has lost most of its mystery and danger. Climbers like Boardman, Tasker, Simpson, and Messner go out looking for a struggle. They find ways of replicating a fight for survival—the insurmountable challenge, the physical agony, the mental steel, the courage to face death—without discovering the underlying purpose that might make it all worthwhile. They say they climb to discover the "new frontiers" of the human mind, to test the limits of endurance, to peer into the deep crevasse of death, but they succeed only in performing a parody of discovery. And in the process, man's age-old struggle against nature is reduced to a staged fight.

It would be wrong to characterize these climbers' efforts as extreme-sport Puritanism. They're after more than purifying agony. What they seek, I think, is the possibility of courage. When Boardman and Tasker take on Changabang, when Reinhold Messner returns to Nanga Parbat, when Stacy Allison pushes up Everest, they place themselves in situations where heroism will be summoned. A century ago they might have battled blizzards or mountain passes in the course of frontier life, but today those hardships are overcome in the comfort of a wide-body jet. Today courage comes in a thousand small decisions and discrete acts; rare is the chance to stand before a Tiananmen Square tank and bask in the bold moment. Even rarer is to stand before a challenge from the natural world, though we crave the chance. And so we induce courage by artificial means.

Mountains are the site of these staged showdowns with nature because they're the place where civilization cannot hold sway. It remains nearly impossible for the human body to survive an extended stay above 20,000 feet. Build a house or hut too high and the mountain will wash it away. We often forget that mountains were once viewed as earthly excrescences. In this age of contaminated urbanity we've made them the very symbol of purity, the last place unblemished by human scratch. We can pour our metaphors onto them, hype the latest "conquest," but we speak more of ourselves than of the hills. The mountain doesn't play games. It sits there, unmoved.

I'd begun my Rainier explorations with a passing interest in the summit. Now I found myself caught between a curiosity urging me to explore the upper mountain and a conscience deeply opposed to the macho ethos of climbing. Having read through thousands of pages of mountain carnage and witnessed the grief brought on by Fischer's death, climbing a mountain could no longer be written off as an innocent lark. Too many questionable motives underlay the whole culture of mountain climbing. Too many people died pursuing goals that were unworthy of their deaths. I didn't want to become one of them.

My father had no such second thoughts. His hints about wanting to climb became larger and more frequent. I put him off by giving him ever more vague reports about my activities on Rainier. I didn't have to veer very far from the truth; the late spring rains combined with my own brooding malaise to keep me away from Rainier for weeks at a time.

In the course of my reading, I came across some four-hundred-year-old advice. Those who would know the world through books, wrote the alchemist Petrus Severinus, deny themselves the sensual experience of their subject. "Burn your books," he wrote, "put on your shoes, climb mountains, explore deserts to gain for yourselves some idea of the things of nature." I'd tacked the quote to the wall above my desk, next to a poster of Rainier in winter. In late spring Severinus's words began gnawing at me; they shamed my armchair mountaineering.

I put away my books and returned to the mountain to see things for myself.

CAMP MUIR

I *began going high.*
    On quiet mornings I slipped out of the city before it awoke and drove to Paradise, snapped on a pair of gaiters, and walked through the mist to the high climbing camp called Camp Muir. I went alone and with others. It takes less than an hour to reach treeline from the parking lot, and from there it's a straight slog up the Muir Snowfield, a two-mile ridge whose undulate tongue runs down the mountain like a carnival slide. Most days I'd crest the last snowrise at one in the afternoon with my shirt floating in sweat. Muir is 10,000 feet high, 4,600 vertical feet from Paradise. Reaching it is like climbing a staircase of 10,000 steps.

Strange things happen up there. One week in June I found the snowfield carpeted with dead insects. Just as entomologist John Edwards had predicted, the snow displayed a massacre of caddisflies, stoneflies, stinkbugs, aphids, mosquitoes, green plant bugs, houseflies, and beetles, all newly hatched and blown up by the wind. A week later I followed the same path and found the crows, ravens, finches, and jays bloated into sloth and the snowfield picked clean.

As spring grew into summer, pollen and dirt soiled the white drifts. Wind funneled up the Nisqually Glacier and crashed into a wall of ice, dropping its load onto the Muir Snowfield and staining it like smoke. If you stand at Panorama Point on a clear day, you might see a cloud create itself from nothing. Moist, warm air from Puget Sound breezes over the glacier, condenses into water vapor, and blows into the Columbia River basin as fully formed cotton. On the snowfield you walk right through it.

High clouds have always fascinated me. My favorite part of a plane ride is the moment when the aircraft cuts into a cloud and everything goes dishwater. As a child growing up in the Pacific Northwest, I assumed this happened on all flights everywhere. If you press your nose against the window you can disorient your mind; your eyes are wide open searching for a focal point, but there's nothing to fix on. It's as if you've stumbled into a dimension where logic, time, and space have been scrambled. Going high on a mountain gives you a chance to climb through the window.

On a good day Camp Muir is as charming as an Arctic weather station: three huts, an A-frame, a two-seat crapper, and a shed. On a bad day it hides under so much snow you could walk right past and never know it was there. People have. The stone blockhouse on your right is a public shelter, cold as a packinghouse, sleeps twenty-five first come first served. A solar toilet sits upwind from the shelter and issues such an acrid reek that some climbers would rather sculpt snow thrones and pack their clinkers out in blue plastic Park Service bags. It's a vast improvement on its predecessors, however. One outhouse used to perch over the Cowlitz Glacier and deliver blasts of freezing air right up the vestibule. Another faced the Muir Snowfield and if you didn't bolt the door, the wind would rip it from its hinges and sail it down the mountain. Three buildings huddle at the base of the rubbly Cowlitz Cleaver: the A-frame ranger hut, a plywood dormitory where Rainier Mountaineering clients pass the night, and RMI's stone cook shack, which has a neat Dutch door and was designed by the famous Seattle architect Carl Gould. Beyond that there's nothing but broken rock and snow. If the moon had snow, it would look a lot like Camp Muir.

Except for the huts, the camp is pretty much the same as when John Muir shivered the night away here in August 1888. The great naturalist was touring the Pacific coast gathering material for a book on the natural wonders of the region. Reaching the summit of Rainier, which was then thought to be the highest mountain in the United States, wasn't in Muir's plans until mountain fever gripped him on his approach. "I did not mean to climb it," he wrote his wife, "but got excited and soon was on top."

The fifty-year-old naturalist arrived in Seattle in a Pullman car with the artist William Keith and his wife, and the three of them stayed as guests of the state attorney general. Muir had no trouble rounding up local climbers for an expedition. The young photographer Arthur Warner scuttled a trip to Alaska to join the expedition when Muir requested his services. A passenger train took the ten-man expedition as far as Yelm, where they packed their supplies onto horses and rode for four days through woods that "arise in shaggy majesty," Muir observed, "every light giving tints of exquisite softness to all the wilderness."

Muir's party loaded small cayuse ponies with "huge, savage packs" that would, he wrote in his journal, make a gypsy caravan look tame and proper in comparison. They took wool blankets, camp stools, tin pots, a camera and tripod, canned food, alpenstocks, steel boot caulks, and rope. They rode horses named Bob Caribou, Dexter, and Bones. They were attacked by a mad grouse.

Muir's Rainier expedition sounds like a roaring ball; the old wilderness writer knew how to have a good time in the woods. He and his mates laughed and joked like boys on a scouting trip. When yellow jackets spooked a horse carrying Arthur Warner's fragile glass photographic plates, Warner shrieked, "Stop him! Oh, my plates! my plates!" which the men considered hysterically funny because they thought he was crying over the tin dinner plates. When rancid butter poisoned their stomachs, the men took it as an opportunity to razz the provisioner. "The canned goods were at first called fresh," Muir recorded, "then in sickness were estimated to be ten years old, and at length, in agony of dyspepsia, their age was measured by centuries and antedated the forests primeval."

Today's two-hour approach from Seattle cost Muir half a week. "By the night of the third day," he wrote, "we reached the Soda Springs [now Longmire] on the right bank of the Nisqually, which goes roaring by, gray with mud, gravel, and boulders from the caves of the glaciers of Rainier, now close at hand." His account of the adventure, published as "An Ascent of Mount Rainier" in the *Pacific Monthly*, became the most famous literary work about Rainier, but the mountain failed to evoke in Muir the kind of passion he felt for his beloved Yosemite. "An Ascent" reads like a climbing-society report—terrain, hardships, success, and a couple of near-fatal slips. But Muir's personal journal reveals an entirely more exciting expedition. There he recorded arguments over the inexperience of a young guide named Joe, penned candid descriptions of the locals (tall, wiry James Longmire "will do anything to earn money"), and grumbled about the local cuisine. In his diary Muir stashed the emotions and reflections that rarely survived the transition to the printed page. Here's where Muir strolled into the evening meadow and listened to the wind murmur through the grass:

> *In all excursions, when danger is realized, thought is quickened, common care buried, and pictures of wild, immortal beauty are pressed into the memory, to dwell forever.*

At seven-thirty on a Monday night in August, John Muir and eight companions stepped up to a small plateau 10,000 feet high on the Cowlitz Cleaver. The men were bushed. They'd been slogging up the snowfield for six hours; most were nauseous from the altitude. Philemon Van Trump, the guide, wanted to press on until Muir, noting that the plateau's sandy pumice suggested shelter from the wind, convinced him to stop for the night. The men erected rock windbreaks around coffin-size beds and softened the dirt by stirring it with pikes. Muir's conjecture proved to be wishful thinking. Heavy winds kept the men's sleep shallow and short. Whether in irony or honor, E. S. Ingraham, namesake of the glacier, dubbed the spot "Camp Muir." Arthur Warner lightened the night's misery by cracking jokes and forcing the men to laugh through their chattering teeth.

The party rose at three the next morning and made the summit by noon. Ingraham charged ahead of Van Trump while Muir coaxed an exhausted companion over the crater rim. Warner set up his camera and captured the first photographs from the summit of Mount Rainier.

Few mountain travelers gathered more joy and wisdom from their high wanderings than John Muir; yet when he reflected upon his Rainier climb, he found little enlightenment and only the narrowest satisfaction. "The view we enjoyed," he wrote, " . . . could hardly be surpassed in sublimity and grandeur, but one feels far from home so high in the sky, so much so that one is inclined to guess that, apart from the acquisition of knowledge and the exhilaration of climbing, more pleasure is to be found at the foot of the mountains than on their frozen tops."

It takes a strong form of mountain love to work at Camp Muir. It takes a strange form of mountain love to work on Camp Muir's toilets. I found both forms in Roger Drake, a quiet fortyish man whose job it is to maintain one of the highest and most expensive outhouses in the world. Every Monday in the summer, he climbs to Camp Muir to empty baskets of shit. One Monday I met him there to talk about it. By the time we rendezvoused in the early afternoon, the mercury had bottomed out at thirty degrees and the wind was blowing like the devil, but it was all the same to Drake, who paid the weather no mind. "I'll show you what we've got," he said as he unhinged the door of the fecal solarium.

A solar toilet is a fancy name for an outhouse with a drying room. "The business," as Roger Drake called it, drops from above into wire baskets lined with a burlap filter. The baskets are housed in a little greenhouse made of clear heavy plastic, which traps the heat of the sun and evaporates the liquid. On days when it's freezing outside, the toilet's holding tank may be a balmy eighty-four degrees. Every couple of weeks, Drake empties the dry pies into forty-gallon drums, which are airlifted off the mountain by helicopters at the end of summer. They're flown to a Tacoma dump, except for the plastic "blue bags," which climbers use as emergency poop-scoopers and which are incinerated as biohazard at a dollar a pound.

The solar toilet at Muir receives about ten thousand visits every year. Drake, who worked in wastewater management before joining the Park Service, doesn't mind the job. It gets him on the mountain a lot—when he's not at Muir he checks the works at Summerland, Panorama Point, Ingraham Flats, and Camp Schurman. "It's kind of like changing a diaper," he said. "Somebody's got to do it."

The buildings at Muir require less upkeep than you'd think. Wood won't rot unless bacteria are present, and few strains can survive at 10,000 feet. Drake's work usually involves fixing a hinge or tightening the spring on the outhouse door. One day he had me test a new spring, and it nearly severed my arm. "Could be a little looser," I told him.

After wiping a foot of snow off the top, Drake pried open the frozen lockbox in which he stored his tools. "Aw, man, the ice is still here."

Eight inches encased a jumble of screwdrivers, hammers, and chisels. "Bummer. I punched a hole in it last time, thinking the water would drain out, but up here it's like the winter that never ended. At least those aren't my good tools."

The toilets and blue bags in which the Park Service requests climbers deposit their waste exist for one simple reason: Shit freezes. It doesn't break down, it doesn't go away. And when seven thousand climbers use the same route every year, the call of nature can't be answered in nature's way without turning the upper mountain into a manure farm.

"Ever pull anything strange out of here?" I asked.

"Well, they say the first rule about sewer systems is that anything that can go in, will go in. The second rule is, anything that can't will too. Somebody said Lou Whittaker was here a few weeks ago and found a headlamp somebody had dropped into the pit toilet. Said it was an eerie glow, like an alien landed in there."

I had to leave because my toes were going numb.

Every campground is a village that shakes out its population each morning, and Camp Muir is more transient than most. The first newcomers arrive about ten-thirty in the morning at the head of a parade that doesn't end until four in the afternoon. Day hikers catch breath and eat lunch in an outcropping of rocks that break the wind and absorb the sun like warming stones. On a clear day the summit can seem tantalizingly close. Rainier's mountainous form all but dissolves at this altitude; the upper glaciers coalesce into a smooth white dome. It's like standing on the lip of a vanilla cone looking up at the scoop.

The day hikers depart by five, leaving the camp to climbers who pitch their tents and settle in for supper and sleep. In the evening a pair of climbing rangers wearing Park Service baseball caps amble through camp making conversation and performing a subtle reconnaissance. They check to see that each party has registered at Paradise and offer advice about route conditions. Hans Andersen, a rookie ranger who first climbed Rainier when he was fourteen, tells four climbers huddled around a boiling pot that the snowbridges are looking dicey. Another exchange about equipment convinces Andersen that these folks know what they're doing. Sometimes people don't. One year an entire family tried to walk across a glacier roped up with a clothesline. Their work done, Andersen and his partner Jennifer Erxleben retreat to the Park Service hut for dinner and a few hours' sleep. Calling their A-frame a hut bestows upon it an undeserved grandiosity. The Butler Hut, named after Rainier's legendary climbing ranger Bill Butler, is as tall as a really tall man and as wide as a not very fat one. It's strapped to the mountain with two half-inch cables, and on the back wall somebody has written IN CASE OF EMERGENCY KICK HERE.

By seven o'clock Andersen and Erxleben's advice has spread like gospel: Everybody's going up the Ingraham direct route and coming down Disappointment Cleaver. Around midnight Andersen and Erxleben leave on a summit climb to check route conditions and help in case rescues are needed. In the public shelter, climbers strap on crampons in the dark and freezing cold and tell each other, "Pretty darn good life, isn't it?" In another hour, warmed by soup and conjoined by rope, they step onto the Cowlitz Glacier and leave care of the village to those of us who stay behind. In the morning we can see them on the mountain's upper dome and they look like fleas on sugar.

If I've given the impression that Camp Muir is a jolly little community, allow me to correct myself. Muir is a microsoviet of cranky, tired, nauseous, scared, anxious, hungry, cold, and often paranoid human beings whose brains are not receiving as much oxygen as they should. They smell bad. Since walking in plastic climbing boots is awkward and taxing, the main activity at Camp Muir is sitting. At 10,000 feet "sharing" is a loaded term. Climbers share supplies within their own expeditions, but tend to look upon requests for food or equipment from neighboring camps much as Davy Crockett might have considered a plea from Santa Ana for spare bullets. Bucking fifty pounds of gear up to Muir is hard work, and requesting a bite of a neighbor's cheese is considered bad form. This isn't to say that most Muirians are stingy; it's just that when you get that high, every piece of equipment becomes crucial to your survival.

Camp Muir mixes the gung-ho with the scared silly, the gearhead with the ill-prepared, the inspirational with the psychotic. Many of the older men in camp are like Lyle, a Tacoma minister who hiked up with a group of buddies, all in their fifties, who planned to tackle the summit a few weeks later. There are out-of-towners like Bob, a Florida cop decked in expensive gear, who spent his summer vacation on the glaciers of Baker and Rainier. There are European climbers who come up alone and wait for days, looking for rope teams that will let them clip in. There are older men like The Commander, the leader of an army reserve unit up for some mountain training. The Commander was a handsome man in his late fifties who dressed for the mountains in the old style: heavy leather boots, fatigue trousers, wool flannel shirt. His men addressed him as Sir and he made grave pronouncements such as "I see no moral advantage in eating instant eggs." Sometimes you meet climbers who embody the phrase *What the hell was he thinking?* People like Ice Axe Einstein, a gentleman who slept away the afternoon in the public shelter trying to decide whether to climb the mountain. He'd come up without an ice axe.

If you spend time at Camp Muir you're likely to meet Ake and Bronka Sundstrom, a retired couple who hike about ten miles every day except when they go grocery shopping, and sometimes even on those days, too. If you meet them you will not overtake them, because they are faster than you. They will pass you. Pleasantly, but they will pass you.

Ake is eighty years old and his wife is seventy-two, which she'll tell you proudly because when you live productively, she'll say, why be ashamed of your age? If you want to know how good or bad the weather was in a given year, Ake and Bronka can tell you according to how many times they made it to Camp Muir. Last year they managed thirty-nine trips, which wasn't bad. Two years ago they went fifty times.

"Everybody thinks we did pretty good this year," Bronka told me, "only I was dying to arrange a go to the fortieth time. But nobody go with me."

"It started up snow, high," explained Ake.

Ake wears eyeglasses so thick that it's tough to tell which eye works and which doesn't (he lost the left one to cancer a few years ago). The legs of old men are not often pretty, but a quarter-century on the trail have turned Ake's into marble limbs that would have enhanced the reputation of Michelangelo. I have stared in awe at another man's legs only twice in my life: once in high school when Rick Fenney, who was later employed as a running back for the Minnesota Vikings, wore a pair of cutoffs in the lunchroom; and again when I saw Ake's eighty-year-old shanks. They are magnificent.

Ake was born in northern Sweden and speaks with a Scandinavian accent that turns *there* into *dare* and *did* into *deed*. I was introduced to him and Bronka by Skip, my snowshoeing companion, and during my time at the mountain I often ran into them on the trail. Some days Skip and I dropped by their house just to hear Ake talk. His words come wrapped in music.

Bronka's tiny frame belies her superhuman endurance. She can blaze up to Camp Muir without stopping for food or pausing in conversation. She requires so little fuel that the act of snacking on the trail seems self-indulgent. Once when I accompanied Bronka to the high camp, she scolded me for stopping to eat and instructed me to suck on a sugarless lozenge the rest of the way. Though her stamina is extraordinary, the quality that Bronka most offers the world is an extreme delight in the possibility of each day. It's as if joie de vivre is a vapor she distills from the mountain air. It made me a little nervous.

Bronka's unflappable cheer seemed all the more curious when I learned her history, which she told me once on the way to Camp Muir. She was born in the twenties in a village south of Kraków, Poland. The Nazis captured her and her parents near the end of the Second World War and sent them to a concentration camp. Her mother and father were killed; Bronka survived. After Allied soldiers liberated her camp, she was sent to a hospital in Stockholm that treated Holocaust survivors. She was eighteen years old. "You lose your parents, you lose everything," she told me. "It leaves you very disturbed. I had a long, long time recovery." At the hospital she met Ake. "He was engaged to a nice Swedish girl," she said. "But he fell in love with me and had all the patience with me. Because I was a mess."

They married and settled in Stockholm, but as the Cold War threatened to turn into a third world war, Bronka told her husband she would not survive another one. He knew she meant it. "Twelve weeks later we were on the boat out of the country." Ake abandoned a promising architectural career for work in construction. "He couldn't get a job in the United States because all the measurements in Sweden were centimeters," Bronka said, "and here by inches and feet. And he didn't have any money to change around. So he just work construction." Ake turned down promotions because the added responsibility would take time from his family.

On the trail to Muir, people sometimes asked Bronka if she didn't tire of walking the same path over and over. "Each time you are in the hills you see things with different eyes," she told them. I asked her how she sustained such optimism as someone who'd witnessed humanity's lowest ebb. How does delight exist in the face of the death camps?

"I had a wonderful Russian psychiatrist in Sweden," she told me. "I was in a group therapy with him. He used to say to us: 'Open the window.' We went open the window. He says, 'How many of you want to jump out?' None of us did. So he says, 'Well, close the window; now we can talk.' At first we thought he was barbaric. But that was our therapy. He said, 'If you hate everybody, you get hate back.' You have to change around."

Ake and Bronka have never climbed to the top of Mount Rainier. The fact so astonished me I had to ask twice. *Never?* "No." RMI guides have entered their names on the summit register in honor of their years on the Muir trail, but they've never gone higher than 10,000 feet.

I suspected some superstition or phobia, but Bronka told me it was simpler than that. "We don't like to stay overnight," she said. "We like to sleep in our own home." Though this seemed like a solvable dilemma—a sunset departure from Paradise would put them on top by dawn—I chose not to press the issue. Perhaps they simply didn't *want* to climb. It flirts with absurdity, the idea of telling a woman who survived the death camps and a man who sacrificed career and country for his family that they have anything to prove. It is enough that they do what they love every day of their lives, walking as far and as freely into the mountain as their legs will take them.

Sometimes when I slept at Camp Muir I'd lie on the shelter bunk and look up at the initials carved in the ceiling post and wonder who put them there.

K.B.

M + P

RWK + JAT

RST "WE WILL SURVIVE"

Something about the immense anonymity of the mountain drives us to mark it. The first white men to climb it planted a brass plaque on the summit. Mountain guides have branded the RMI shack: "ERSHLER 71-75, 76, 77" and "VAN HOY 79." Phil Ershler has been to the summit more than three hundred times; in 1981 Craig Van Hoy set the record for a Paradise-to-summit run by completing the round trip in five hours and twenty minutes. When he reached the

Park Service register on Columbia Crest, the mountain's highest point, Van Hoy wrote, "Praise the Lord!"

That and other climbers' dicta are kept by the U.S. government at the federal records archive in Seattle. I was curious to read the thoughts of climbers at 14,000 feet, to see how they wanted to be remembered to the mountain, so I pulled some registers from the archive—I chose 1991 and, for a round fifty-year comparison, 1941—and spent an afternoon browsing through other people's experiences.

The 1941 register was just that—a register of names on 4-by-6 cards. Though the Park Service form included comment lines, few are filled out. The 1941 register contains the clipped speech and quaint slang of the era, and in its short comments reveals something else: the absence of personal glory.

> Jim Beebe, July 20, 1941: Fooey.
>
> Bob Powell, July 20: Cold as the devil
>   Also a heck of a long hike
>
> Bob Glantel, age 22, Aug 2, 1941: Too much wind. I'm
>   leaving.
>
> b. H. Britten, age 24, Bayonne, NJ Aug 11 1941: Damn
>   tired.
>
> Dee Molenaar, Age 23, August 24, 1941: Cold as hell!
>   Arrived 5:30AM 10-1/2 hrs from Paradise
>
> Lene H. Brigham Jr., age 21, August 24, 1941: Killed on
>   Russell Glacier 8-10-41. Ashes brought here
>   8-24-41. W. McClure Jr, leader.

Fifty years later Rainier's summiteers had turned into literary exhibitionists. Climbers thank their friends and loved ones in nicknames and catchphrases. Personal milestones are marked—a first climb, a fortieth birthday, a moment of silence for partners who died before they could climb Rainier. RMI guides mark their latest climb in rhyme; muscle fatigue, mental lassitude, and hand-chilling cold are reflected in unpunctuated sentences, misspelled words, and the poor decision to paraphrase Led Zeppelin at 14,000 feet. And through many comments comes the constant chorus of our age: Hey everybody, look at me!

> 7/1/91 NPS Rangers begin new log book on a super summit day 5:20am departed Muir at 11:30. Great sunrise on a warm 27 degree F. Ya all take care - 'Climb if you will, but do it safe!' -Steve Winslow

> 7/2/91 Tim Kinshn In loving memory of my father who tried but never made the sumit. He his always on tops with me.

> July 3, 1991 Kevin Slotterbeck RMI #23

> John Erben #1
> We have snowboards in hand and hope to make this the first snowboard descent from the high point of crater via Emmons.
> MAJOR SHRED ON!

> Fourth of July!!!
> RMI Camp Muir Seminar
> Geo Dunn #279 sure felt fine
> I'm still second in line
> But the record will soon be mine

7/5/91 A long time dream come true - I have trust in my
fellow man and faith in God...together it happens!
Thanks Steve Thanks Pete (I hear your voice each step!)
Judy Knudthon

7-6-91 my mom did it in the 1930s! So I had to do it too.
Maybe someday my daughter can read this. It's fun to
wave home from here! Dana Gross Portland OR

7-7-91 Mike Gauthier - Schurman climbing Ranger up
for 1st time this yr - 5 hr 50 min - not bad for 1st
time of season - "Gimme paw!"

7/7/91 Ed Hrivnak - Tacoma Mountain Rescue
304th Air Rescue Squadron
"We are norsemen, hardy and bold
we mount the black waves in
our doughty sleek ships and
go - araiding.
We are norsemen, cold as stone.
(Gary and Kenny are wimps)

7-7-91 Jason M. Schroedel
Well I'm nine years old this is the highest peak I've
ever climbed the only other glacier peak I've climbed
is Hood, Well Bye.

7/7/91 12:53 pm George J. Carman
Put me back onto the mountain
I am climb-to-the-stars

7/26/91 Peter Taylor
"All that glitters is snow as the view from the city is
deceiving...and she's buying a stairway to Heaven"

As agreed over 24 years ago, I hereby add to this register
the names of those with whom I climbed via the

Nisqually Icefall route to the summit of Mount Rainier on June 1, 1967. The climbers in our party were as follows:

* Jerry Clark
* Hank Janes
* Mark McLaughlin
* John Russell
* Steve Taylor
  Kim Turley
  Joe Wilcox

*Deceased in a climbing accident July 1967 on Mt McKinley (along with climbing companions Dennis Luchterhand and Walt Taylor).

       Kim Turley 8/22/91

I asked the archivist if I could photocopy this one. He said he thought it would be okay:

One of my last nights at Camp Muir I woke at one a.m. and walked outside to lie on the moonlit snow. Ten thousand feet closer to heaven than home, the stars shone as if making their empyrean debut. High altitude wiped away the atmospheric scum and presented a view clean as a NASA still: three dimensions of cold, gassy, and dark. A phrase Bronka had given me came to mind: "Stars so big you think they are houses." So many twinkles milked up the sky that constellation spotting was a needle-and-haystack job: Ursa Major, bear of the heavens, stood poised to eat the head of Boötes the plowman; Draco the dragon breathed fire at Hercules; Leo and Virgo reclined near the horizon, away from the dogs, lyres, horses, crowns, and fish junking up the universe. Space hardware floated so evenly over the Earth that I tried to find a metaphor for the smoothness of satellites but could imagine nothing so steady as the things themselves. So an hour passed. I lay prone on the ice, eyes open, vision blurring with tears. There were moments on the mountain when I approached a perfect understanding of why I had come, and one occurred that night. As the universe spun above me, I breathed in the exhaled blood of high hemlocks and listened to the glaciers turn in their beds and saw the same forces create the same moment on mountains miles and days down the continent. That night Mount Rainier had my soul alone as witness to its fleeting benevolence, a single intruder lying on the ice reveling in the complete act of existence.

An hour later the wind had calmed. The light creak-and-bang of the outhouse door provided a backdrop of white noise, punctuated by the cry of a climber pleading with his partner to rise and climb: "Get up! Geeet up!" The glow of a half-million people—Portland, Oregon— backlit the barnacle of Mount St. Helens. Behind me, bootcrunch: A final patrol of mountaineers trudged joylessly across the Cowlitz Glacier like a shift of miners following their headlamps. They left me with the stars, full and content.

When I told my father about going to Camp Muir, he immediately wanted to join me on a trip. "You're still thinking about climbing, right?" Sure, I mumbled. I wasn't completely lying. My experiences at Muir had pulled me back from the mountain funk I'd fallen into after Scott Fischer's death. Ake and Bronka convinced me there still was joy to be found in the high hills. And they'd shown me I didn't have to climb to find it. Beside that, though, sat the simple desire to see what was up there.

"If you go up, I want to go with you," my father said.

We'd talked about climbing Rainier off and on since high school, but always in a maybe-next-summer kind of way. This time I sensed he meant it.

"Are you serious?"

"I'm fifty-five years old. When am I going to get another chance?"

Over the next weeks and months, I gave him room to back out gracefully. I pointed out the rigors of the trip, the training he'd need to do, the cost of a guided climb.

"You're sure?" I said.

"You got us booked yet?" he said.

I booked us.

THAT HELL-TAINTED AIR

O nce I thought I saw red algae growing on the snow at Camp Muir, but when I picked at it I realized it was somebody else's vomit. If you flew straight from Muir to Puget Sound and dropped a measuring tape, it would fall just short of two miles. At that altitude commercial jets are fully pressurized, because the air contains more than one-quarter less oxygen than at sea level. At the summit, almost a full mile higher, every breath draws one-third less oxygen than normal. The body responds to this in a variety of ways. Most are unpleasant. During a typical morning, at least half the climbers on Rainier's glaciers contract symptoms of Acute Mountain Sickness (AMS). One symptom is,

you throw up. The act of emesis is an experience shared by mountaineers the world 'round. At their 10,000-foot camp a member of
John Muir's expedition contracted such violent AMS that it drove him
beyond caring about the cold; he would have frozen to death had
others not looked after him. Joseph Barcroft, the British pioneer in respiratory illness, noted that the very predictability of AMS gave rise to
the study of high-altitude disease. "Most persons as they approached
the snow line in the Alps were inclined to vomit," he wrote. "Sometimes the inclination overcame them."

Ice and falling rock aren't the only hazards deterring high mountain
travel. The air itself is against you.

On weekends Camp Muir becomes a mountain sickness ward. "I'm
still feeling a little barfy," one climber tells his companion. "S'pose I
could borrow an aspirin?" asks a headachey fellow. (Curiously, pain
relievers were among the few supplies climbers at Muir offered,
unprompted, to strangers.) Two men charge into camp on a Saturday
morning. "Whee-ew, I'm a little dizzy," says the lead man. "That's what
happens when you hike up without stopping *at all*," replies his partner.
Most climbers on Rainier go too high too fast. Traveling from Seattle's
sea level to 14,000 feet in less than two days is an ascent rate seven
times faster than that recommended for the prevention of AMS. The
climbing rangers usually become acclimatized after the second week
of the summer season, but sometimes you can't predict. A few years
ago a group of geologists had to abort a costly study on the summit
crater when the ranger who'd flown up with them started hurling from
the altitude. He was embarrassed.

He shouldn't have been. Altitude sickness strikes without fear or
favor. Todd Burleson, who's been guiding on high mountains for more

than twelve years, still feels its effects when he goes above 9,000 feet. Mountain sickness can scuttle a summit climb or turn the tide of war. During the 1962 border conflict between China and India, Indian troops rushed to the high borderlands and fell in alarming numbers to mountain sickness. The Chinese army, whose soldiers acclimatized during a slow, steady ascent, had far fewer losses.

The ancients knew mountain air was bad, they just didn't know why. In some regions the blame was placed on antimony, a silver-white metal; in others the vapors of rhubarb and roses were suspect. The air near the top of Mount Olympus was said to be so thin that the ancient Greeks held sponges soaked in water and vinegar over their noses. The *Tseen Han Shoo*, an ancient Chinese history, refers to the Great Headache Mountain and the Little Headache Mountain as places where "men's bodies become feverish, they lose color and are attacked with headaches and vomiting." In Tibet the sickness was called *damgiri*, meaning "breath seizing," or *dugri,* poison of the mountain; in Turkey, *esh*, a miasma; in northern India, *bishkahawa*, poisonous air. When the Moguls invaded Tibet in 1532, *damgiri* gave them no end of trouble. Sultan Said Khan, a pious and merciful Muslim who made war on the infidel Tibetans because they were infidel Tibetans, proved exceptionally susceptible to the disease. We know this because his lieutenant, Mirza Muhammad Haidar, who once boasted of exterminating "the whole army of Kashmir and the kings," took advantage of his retirement to write a history of the Mogul conquests. The Khan overran Tibet with a force of five thousand men, whose misery provided us with one of the earliest and most complete catalogues of symptoms. "In every case one's breath so seizes him that he becomes exhausted, just as if he had run up a steep hill with a heavy burden on his back," wrote Haidar. "On account of the oppression it is difficult to sleep. Should, however, sleep overtake one, the eyes are hardly closed before one is awoke with a start caused by the oppression on the lungs and chest." Some of the Khan's men turned senseless; others talked nonsense or lost the power of speech entirely. Those who suffered swollen hands and feet, Haidar observed, usually died "between dawn and breakfast time." One day the men rode their horses hard without considering the altitude. The next morning they awoke to two thousand dead horses.

High altitude nearly killed the Khan on his first journey into Tibet ("his constitution, undermined by excessive drinking, proved less vigorous than his religious zeal," wrote his tactful subordinate). After passing a winter there, he was anxious to return home. Unfortunately, Haidar noted, "this second journey across the heights, achieved for him what the first had so nearly accomplished." While crossing an icy 17,000-foot Himalayan pass, "a grave change for the worse took place in the Khan's condition, from the effects of that hell-tainted air." He never recovered. Soon after the Khan crossed the pass, "his pious soul took flight to the regions of the blessed." Haidar did not record whether the Khan died of the disease or its cure, which in sixteenth-century Tibet consisted of slicing open a wound at the hairline.

We live at the bottom of an ocean of air. The metaphor belongs to Evangelista Torricelli, a student of Galileo who invented the mercury barometer in 1643. A few months after creating the instrument Torricelli dashed off a letter to a colleague in which he described our atmospheric condition. "We live," he wrote, "submerged at the bottom of an ocean of the element air, which by unquestioned experiments is known to have weight." That ocean is mostly nitrogen (seventy-eight percent) and oxygen (twenty-one percent), with molecules of argon, carbon dioxide, neon, helium, ozone, and hydrogen floating in the mix, along with specks of sea salt, dust, pollen, smoke, bacteria, volcanic ejections, and meteoric fragments. The proportion of nitrogen, oxygen, and other gases remains constant up to about 80,000 meters, ten times higher than the highest mountains on Earth. What wreaks havoc with human flesh is the changing pressure under which those gases exist.

Proving that the atmosphere has weight is as easy as running your hand through the air. Something is *there;* we feel it rush over our skin. At high speed its weight knocks down trees, tosses freighters, tears houses apart. Nitrogen and oxygen molecules provide most of the mass. Their molecular weights—twenty-eight and thirty-two, respectively—are fourteen and sixteen times heavier than hydrogen. This is why hydrogen balloons rise. At the bottom of Torricelli's ocean, the air we breathe at sea level is compressed by the cubic miles of air sitting on top of it. The higher the altitude, the lighter the weight of the overlying atmosphere. The barometric pressure at sea level is 760 torr, a unit of measure named after Torricelli. By 10,000 feet the pressure has dropped to 525 torr, and at the 14,410-foot summit of Mount Rainier the pressure is around 440 torr, or more than forty percent less than at sea level. Most of the air collects at the bottom of the troposphere. When you stand atop Mount Rainier, almost half the weight of the world's air floats beneath you.

Think of the lungs as a pair of bellows. Muscles between the ribs pull the lung walls apart, drawing in outside air. Red blood cells pick up oxygen from the lungs and deliver it to the heart. Because of the lower atmospheric pressure at high altitude, the blood delivers less O_2 to the heart and the body becomes hypoxic—deprived of oxygen.

Even with a full lungful, the body doesn't receive a normal shot of oxygen. Breathe deeply at sea level. Breathe deeply at the summit. Feels like the same full serving of air, but at 14,000 feet the volume of air that filled the lungs at sea level has expanded (because there's less weight pressing it down), and now takes up forty percent more space. The lungs remain the same size, so every time you fill the tank you're taking in forty percent less air, and forty percent less oxygen. A plastic bottle capped with the thin air of the summit and taken to sea level will buckle as if crushed by a truck.

To compensate for the lower pressure and oxygen content, mountain climbers often practice pressure breathing, blowing and sucking in a hyperventilating wheeze. Pilots in the Second World War learned the technique in case their oxygen cut out. They called it "grunt breathing." Although Rainier guides swear by the practice, medical researchers aren't convinced that they're accomplishing anything. "We studied it on Denali and found it had no physiologic or performance benefit whatsoever," said Robert Schoene, a pulmonary specialist who's climbed and conducted high-altitude research on mountains all over the world. "It's a fatuous technique that may have only some psychologic, meditative, rhythmic benefit." The only real antidote to mountain sickness is time. After a few days at high altitude the body will produce more red blood cells to compensate for the oxygen shortage. Since my trips to Camp Muir were one- and two-day affairs that never allowed me to acclimatize, I grunt-breathed my way up (medical research be damned) and popped Advil like it was candy.

When Barcroft began charting the effects of "oxygen want" in the early twentieth century, he noted that *damgiri* victims resembled stumbling drunks. Slurred speech and the staggers (ataxia, in the medical journals) are just two things that happen when the body is deprived of oxygen. Among the stranger effects of high altitude is bleeding lips, which affected Alexander von Humboldt during his 1802 trek up Chimborazo, and Lou Whittaker during his 1975 assault on K2. Sleep comes fitfully, and sleeping breath may be drawn rapidly and then quit for a few seconds. When the nineteenth-century English physicist John Tyndall fell asleep during an ascent of Mont Blanc, his tentmate panicked and shook him awake. "You quite frighten me," Tyndall's partner said. "I listened for some minutes and have not heard you breathe once."

Lack of oxygen also affects our dreams. "A common nightmare at high altitude," one researcher reported, "is that the tent has been covered with snow by an avalanche and the subject wakes violently feeling suffocated and very short of breath." As a night vision, this is especially disturbing because it is so often the case that the tent has, in fact, been covered with snow by an avalanche and is suffocating its tenants.

Once you go above 10,000 feet, altitude problems can turn far more serious than AMS headaches. Top of the list is high-altitude pulmonary edema (HAPE), a condition in which the blood thickens, the skin turns blue, the lungs fill with fluid, and, at the farthest reach from the sea, you drown. High-altitude cerebral edema (HACE) runs a close second: The brain swells and causes massive headaches, fumbly coordination, slurred speech, irrational behavior, and eventual collapse. The only remedy is to go down or die. HAPE and HACE fatalities usually occur on remote mountains higher than Rainier, but the conditions aren't unknown in the Cascades. A few times each summer a climber stumbles into Camp Muir with a mild form of HAPE or HACE, although in the last few years the more serious cases have come from the smaller (12,276-foot) Mount Adams. In one instance a climber had to be airlifted off Adams after falling into an edema-induced coma; in another, a young climber died at 9,000 feet.

"You want to know how altitude messes with your head," a ranger told me, "you ought to get in touch with Jim Litch." Litch, a physician and former climbing ranger at Rainier, practiced high-altitude medicine at Mount McKinley and in the Himalayas. After failing to reach him, I let my phone messages simmer for a couple of months. The next time Litch reached an outpost civilized enough to patch him through to his voice mail, he called me back. That's often how it is with people who work in the mountains. Your call will be returned, but it may have to wait until the next yak convoy crosses the pass.

"Everyone is suffering from lack of oxygen at extreme elevation," Litch told me. "Everyone has impaired judgment. A lot of commercial guides and climbers can climb well at heights under 7,000 meters (22,966 feet), but those same people are fooling themselves above 8,000 meters." On the Earth's highest peaks, the epistemological question—How do we know what we know?—assumes life-threatening importance. In the high Himalayas and Karakorams, climbers versed in mountain medicine might know that mental agility deteriorates with every passing hour, but their own crumbling minds would keep them from realizing that their own minds were crumbling. "It's like a drunk leaving a party saying, 'Listen, I know I'm drunk but I can drive. I'm fine,'" Litch said.

I'd been thinking about Scott Fischer's state of mind, and so had Litch. The week Fischer died Litch had been climbing Ama Dablam, a Himalayan peak about twenty-five miles from Everest. He and his partners attempted a quick Alpine-style push up the southwest ridge of Ama Dablam, but the unstable weather pushed them below their high camp. They sat in a lower camp for two days watching the wind whip up horsetails of snow on the summit. On the third day they descended to base camp and received a message that more than twenty people were missing on Everest.

Litch's experience on Everest the previous year had convinced him that even the most experienced mountaineers could lose their minds in thin air. His line of ascent had taken him up the North Ridge, a tougher route than the South Col because of its exposed rock and the jet stream blasts that South Col climbers, protected by Lhotse, encounter only in the last few hundred meters to the summit. When Litch and his two partners reached the top of Everest, they reveled in the brilliant windless weather. "I told people it was so calm I could have lit a match," he recalled. A few weeks later when he viewed slides from the trip, he realized how badly his senses had failed him. His snapshots showed banners starched by the wind. More evidence turned up on a tape of the conversation between base camp and the summit party. Litch's climbing partner announced the team's successful ascent to an excited base crew and then handed the radio to Litch. "Hold on, here's Jim," he said. Litch recalled raising the radio to his mouth and being cut off before he could get a word out. "Jim! Jim! Are you there?" the base operator asked. "What's going on?" Litch, taken aback, thought. "What's *your* problem? Cool your jets." Later, he was shocked to hear himself on tape. The broadcast began with Litch's climbing partner relaying greetings to the base crew before passing the radio to Litch. There followed three minutes of radio silence. Finally the base operator asked, "What's going on up there? Where's Jim?" Litch, sounding annoyed, answered, "*Here's* Jim." And the radio lapsed back into silence.

Hallucinations are another familiar feature of Everest climbs. Climbers report sharing the ascent with ghost partners; some even break rations with them. One researcher who studied climbers at Everest's 17,000-foot base camp found that lack of oxygen dulls the brain's higher functions first; it's part of the body's built-in survival mechanism. Basic functions like breathing are the last to go. The early effects of oxygen depletion are felt in the basal ganglia region, which controls tongue, lip, and larynx motion and the ability to make sound judgments. Just when we need them most, perception and judgment nod off. Tom Hornbein, the anesthesiologist and high-altitude specialist who designed the oxygen masks that his teammates wore on the 1963 American Everest expedition, worried that during his climb of Everest's West Ridge it wouldn't be a question of having enough breath to inflate his air mattress at 26,000 feet—he wasn't sure he'd remember *how* to blow it up.

At 29,000 feet the air delivers two-thirds less oxygen to the lungs than at sea level. When Reinhold Messner and Peter Habeler climbed Everest without supplemental oxygen in 1978, breathing consumed the climbers' minds. Standing at the top of the world, Messner imagined himself as "nothing more than a single, narrow gasping lung." Researchers who tested mountaineers going above 8,000 meters found that thin air often impaired concentration and induced short-term memory loss and a diminution of "cognitive flexibility" (that is, it dulled a nimble mind). The mind crumbles even with the aid of O_2 tanks. Scientists reported that mountaineers high on Everest who climb with supplemental oxygen "may behave similar to an individual with a known acute organic brain syndrome." They fumble like victims of brain damage. During postsummit tests in Kathmandu, some climbers wrote "warning" as "warninG"; gave 49, 52, and 57 as the multiple of 17 and 3; spelled triangle "trangle"; and pronounced Episcopal "Ekpiscopal." Eric Shipton, who led the 1953 British expedition to Everest, recalled a bout of altitude-induced aphasia on an earlier expedition in his memoir *Upon that Mountain*. "If I wished to say 'give me a cup of tea,' I would say something entirely different—maybe 'tram-car, cat, put,'" he wrote. "I was perfectly clear-headed . . . but my tongue just refused to perform . . . "

Far from warning others away from mountains, I think Shipton's and Litch's experiences added to their allure. The impulse to climb mountains isn't that much different from the curiosity that drives some people to explore space and others to drop acid. It's the search for the strange. Mountains like Rainier are doubly tantalizing because they're such a common part of our personal landscape and yet they sustain such an otherworldly environment. A person could freeze to death, gasping for air, in a summit storm while Seattleites watered their lawns and admired the mountain view. It ain't like here, up there.

The limit of survivable altitude has yet to be found. Eighteenth-century scientists believed a night at 11,000 feet would kill a man until Horace Bénédict de Saussure spent two days at a high Alpine pass. (De Saussure would have stayed longer had guides not stolen his wine.)

Everest without oxygen was thought madness until Messner and Habeler proved it sane. Climbers often refer to heights above 25,000 feet as "the death zone," because the body can't replenish the energy it burns at that altitude. But the body has remarkable adaptive powers. Some Tibetan nomads live near 15,000 feet, and miners in the northern Chilean Andes live in iron huts 19,516 feet above the sea. Every Sunday the miners descend to play a soccer match at 13,776 feet.

Some of the earliest altitude deaths were recorded by eighteenth- and nineteenth-century balloonists, who faced the constant peril of floating too high to breathe. On April 15, 1875, Gaston Tissandier and two colleagues ascended from Paris in the balloon *Zenith* to conduct meteorological research. Tissandier fainted at 26,500 feet, and when he revived he found the balloon descending and his companions dead from asphyxiation. The *Zenith* had topped out at 27,950 feet, more than a thousand feet below Everest, yet the atmosphere killed two men doing nothing more strenuous than sitting. Since Tissandier's day scientists have discovered that with time, the body can adapt to the Earth's most extreme altitude. Messner and his partner Peter Habeler were able to climb Everest breathing the available air because their bodies adapted to the high environment over a period of weeks and months. Had they ballooned up from sea, the climbers would have passed out in less than two minutes. Their long trek through Nepal and measured climb up the mountain allowed the pressure of oxygen in their blood to increase in response to the lower pressure of oxygen in the air. The body trains itself to deal with the oxygen shortage. Elite climbers often take advantage of this acclimatization to climb two peaks in succession. During his pursuit of all fourteen of the world's 8,000-meter summits, Ed Viesturs, a world-class mountaineer who began as an RMI guide, planned to use this piggyback strategy to climb Everest and then immediately move on to nearby Manaslu while his blood was still revving high. (Viesturs summited on Everest a couple of weeks after Scott Fischer's death, but ran out of time before he could attempt Manaslu.)

Could we climb a mountain higher than Everest? Possibly—but not much higher. In the 1920s Barcroft believed a human being could acclimatize up to 29,000 feet; his successors aren't so sure. An experiment conducted by the U.S. Navy in 1946 to find the limits of survivable height used a decompression chamber to subject several men to an atmospheric pressure 18 torr lower than the pressure on Everest. Forty years later volunteers in a similar experiment survived for more than four hours in a simulated 29,000-foot environment. The absolute limit might exist somewhere between 30,000 and 40,000 feet.

In his medical aviation history *The Dangerous Sky*, Douglas Robinson evaluated the likelihood of a human being surviving a rise through the troposphere. Beyond 30,000 feet, low air pressure would release nitrogen from its solution in the bloodstream and body fluids. The nitrogen would collect in bubbles, Robinson wrote, "like those in a soda bottle whose cap is released." Divers know this as the bends, which happens when they rise too fast from deep water. Symptoms caused by the bubbles, Robinson wrote, "range from the annoying itching and crawling sensations under the skin, pain in joints wherein the bubbles would feel like gravel, to the serious 'chokes,' a sensation of suffocating with dry coughing, caused by bubbles in the lung circulation, and from bubble formation in blood vessels of the brain causing headache, paralysis, convulsions, and death." Climbers might be able to reach a 40,000-foot peak if they inhaled pure oxygen all the way. But at 50,000 feet the barometric pressure reaches 87 torr, at which point even pure oxygen can't save you. Carbon dioxide and water vapor in the lungs would expand to fill both chambers, leaving no room for oxygen. If by some miracle you floated alive to 63,000 feet, you would reach the terrifying "Armstrong Line," the point at which the atmospheric pressure, 47 torr, equals the pressure of water vapor at 98.6 degrees Fahrenheit. At the Armstrong Line the blood and body fluids boil.

MEADOW STOMPING

The Paradise valley stays snowbound for so long that the springtime melt seems contrary to the natural order. Between October and May, fifteen feet of snow smothers the subalpine park that sits 6,000 feet high on the mountain's southern slope. Come June the snow escapes in watery veins that feed the Paradise River, which joins the Nisqually River, which expires in the running tides of Puget Sound, which flushes into the deep conclusion of the Pacific. Thin islands of rock appear in May, and by June they've broadened into little Australias, their rotten stems matted like tide grass. Meltwater running beneath the snow isn't warm enough for most plants, but the avalanche and glacier lilies can sip it cold. Their green shoots slip through the muddy weave and melt the last frosting of snow with the warmth of their own bodies.

This intrusion of color accelerated week by week as I passed through the valley on my way to Camp Muir, and brought on feelings of frustration and regret. Next to the glory of autumn, winter is my favorite season. Its cold darkness drives us indoors to cherish small pleasures: coffee, books, wool socks, conversation. Summer is common; winter is rare. For nine months the mountain held the constancy of winter and granted me the illusion of stopped time, allowed me to keep studs on my tires until a Seattle cop pulled me over and ordered them off.

As the land continued to rise, the snow retreated to shady nooks beneath subalpine firs. I felt an urge to stomp the islands down, stay the spring, save the snow. But the land rose faster and faster until one day I drove to Paradise and witnessed summer's full victory. The meadows had arrived.

In Lummi Indian legend Mount Rainier deserted her husband, Mount Baker, and took all the fruits and flowers with her. On August afternoons when the wind brushes swales of yellow glacier lilies, lavender asters, shaggy white anemones, delicate bells of pink and white heather, and the flamelick heads of red paintbrush, you feel the legend couldn't be anything but true. The display awed even John Muir, who called the Paradise valley "the most extravagantly beautiful of all the alpine gardens I ever beheld in all my mountain-top wanderings." There are more flowers here than any one mountain could bear.

Between John Muir's day and ours, the meadows were nearly ground into dust. In the park's early years the idea was to use the meadows, not conserve them. Turn-of-the-century vacationers rode pack horses up the Paradise Road and relaxed in one of the commercial tent camps that spilled over the valley. Automobiles displaced horses after the First World War and ferried a higher class of tourist to the Paradise Inn, a magnificent mountain chalet made from old-growth fir.

By the 1920s Paradise had become a destination resort boasting two hundred seventy-five cabins, a laundry, an ice cream plant, a photo shop, a boys' camp, and a horse corral. Motorists drove to their tents across fragile fields of huckleberry and heather. For laughs, campers set matches to groves of subalpine firs and watched the bonfires roar. A local motorcycle club once invited two hundred fifty cyclists to tear up the meadows in a hill climb contest. The patience of park officials seemed to find its limit with the bikers. Park Superintendent O. A. Tomlinson banished the club from the park for, among other things, executing suicidal passes on the Paradise Road and gunning their engines "seemingly for the purpose of making as much noise as possible."

This was the era when national parks were run like amusement parks. The Rainier National Park Company, which ran the park's various concessions, was forever cooking up new schemes to draw tourists. One summer the Park Company hired a group of Yakama Indians to give talks, sell trinkets, and generally "act Indian" in and around Paradise. The Yakamas, however, were more interested in racing horses and picking berries than leading singalongs; they were fired after one season.

Paradise fever reached its peak in 1931 when the Park Company constructed a nine-hole golf course on the meadows. Players teed off near the Paradise Inn and played the entire nine downhill. A shuttle bus returned them to the clubhouse. The fact that snow covered the course until July, and that golf is a game played with a tiny white ball,

failed to deter the park planners. After a few short seasons and count-
less lost balls, the course was returned to wildflowers.

This commercial activity was catastrophic for the meadows. In the
National Park library at Longmire there is a photograph of a young
woman visiting the Paradise valley in the 1920s. Wearing a cloche that
perfectly rims her bangs, she poses before an alarmingly smooth
meadow. The hills look as though they've been shorn by a flock of
sheep. The same spot today would gladden a conservator's heart:
uneven, clumpy, shin-deep in flowers. What happened in the interim
was a mass banishment of tents, horses, motorcycles, five-irons, laun-
derers, ice creameries, and wandering bipeds. Rainier botanists have
carried out a restoration program since the mid-1980s that has
reseeded and transplanted more than 100,000 plants. It's taken nearly
a century to revive the splendor of John Muir's 1888.

I liked the idea of a national park greenhouse even before I saw it. The
audacity—raising a 235,000-acre garden from seed! The operation
turned out to be less than I'd imagined, of course. Ann Bell, the park
horticulturist, took me on a tour of her operation, which was contained in two modest structures in an empty field behind the park's
administrative headquarters in Ashford.

Bell's hothouse is a botanical preemie ward. She plants seeds and
fiber-thin clippings in Dixie cups and nurses them for years before
revegetation crews transplant the not-very-much-bigger plants to old
campsites, horse ruts, and hiking trails. The flowers and forbs are so
tiny it's sometimes hard to see them at all. In the largest greenhouse,
Bell readied mountain daisies no bigger than candle flames for a mass

transplant in the former Paradise campground. They'd come this far from seed in four months. In the meadow, Bell told me, it would've taken four years, if they had germinated at all. "On a lot of sites the conditions are so harsh that the seed can't even get there," she said. "The winds aren't blowing in the right direction or the site is too eroded. It might even take hold, but if the sun comes out for a week, it's so hot and exposed up there that the seed will die."

The mountain daisy is a nimble sprouter compared to its meadow neighbors. As Bell and I walked from the greenhouse into an outdoor garden, she pointed out fifteen thousand huckleberry seedlings, the pre-est of the preemies. Peering into the soil cup, I needed a moment to spot the plant—there it was, dwarfed by a fungus gnat. It had been growing for six months. Even at this low altitude, it takes three years to bring huckleberries and heathers to a transplant-ready three inches tall.

Subalpine plants are so finely adapted to their surroundings that Bell must take extraordinary precautions to keep them from adapting to the luxuries of low elevation. She bent down to examine a sprig of red heather. "You could fertilize to get them to grow quicker, but that would change the plant," she said. If the shrub grew faster, the nodes between its leathery leaves would be too long. Heather needs compact, dense growth to survive the hard life up high; the heavy snow load would kill any leggy growth. "I try to stress out the plants so they can make it in the meadows," Bell explained.

We're awed by the antiquity of trees, but the botanical world is filled with ancients ignored because they subsist below our feet. University of Washington botanist Ola Edwards once tested the age of Rainier's subalpine heather communities by carbon-dating remnant stems and analyzing pollen found in ash layers. Her research led her to believe that the heather's genetic line stretched back ten thousand years. In part because of Edwards's work, park botanists are meticulous about preserving the genetic integrity of the sites they restore. Plants contain unique genetic codes that allow them to survive in particular environments. A plant adapted to a cool shady spot might wither and die in an exposed site five yards away. Seeds and cuttings used to revegetate a barren patch are taken from plants nearby that have adapted to the microclimate.

It's tempting to take a bushel of cuttings from a single healthy shrub, but you'd only end up with a meadow of clones. "You want twenty to thirty different genotypes out there," park botanist Regina Rochefort told me. Genetic diversity is one of a plant species' main defenses against extinction. One strain may die of disease, cold, wind, or thirst, but its neighbor, blessed with a more amenable genetic code, will live to propagate future generations. The Irish learned the hard truth of this principle in 1845, when blight attacked a potato crop which had descended from uniform genetic stock that was unresistant to the disease. The blight destroyed a nation's harvest, and half a million people starved.

Petal by needle by stem, the subalpine meadow holds verities about the life of the mountain. During summer its Renoir pastels hold brief advantage over the ice and rock in their struggle to define the mountain. A single flower captures the tenacity and fragility of life on the Earth's high ridges. Its roots nest under snow for ten months before bursting out for a glorious eight-week run. The first frost of September kills its shoots and the cycle begins again.

The mountain is never devoid of life. Grasses and sedges survive in rock fissures as high as ten thousand feet, and mosses and liverwort thrive in the steam vents of the summit crater. Lichens are so hardy that scientists use them to track the historical movement of glaciers. The same heathers whose genetic ancestry stretches back ten thousand years are so frail that a troop of Boy Scouts could wipe out fifty years of growth in two minutes' passing. In the harsh world of the high mountain, the meadows are a compensation of rainbows after the frozen flood. They exemplify, as Edward Abbey once said of a cactus flower, better than the rose among thorns the unity of opposites. They are acts of kindness in the midst of war.

Some time after I spoke with Ann Bell, I offered myself for reveg duty. I joined a group of forty volunteers on a torn strip of valley not far from the Paradise Inn. Regina Rochefort had hoped to put us to work higher up near the alpine zone around Panorama Point, but a heavy mist socked in the valley and she didn't want to lose anybody wandering onto the Nisqually Glacier. We planted two acres of mountain daisies and cinquefoils and sprigs of sedges an inch at a time. The plants reminded me of sprouts on a sandwich; if you weren't careful, you could kill them with a pinch.

Once Ann Bell's plants reach the meadow, it's Bill Dengler's job to keep them out from under the boot heels. When I met Dengler, the park's chief naturalist, in his Longmire office, the first thing he did was dip into a bucket and hand me a button that read "Don't Be a Meadow Stomper." I pinned it to my jacket, feeling like a visitor to the Ford White House during the "Whip Inflation Now" days. Outside of murder, meadow stomping is about the worst thing you can do in Mount Rainier National Park. Every summer the flowers bloom and every summer thousands of heels grind them away. It drives the rangers crazy. The park has even commissioned studies of the problem. One group of researchers worked up a profile of the typical off-trail trespasser, the way the FBI profiles serial killers. (The most common stompers: teenagers.) Others tested signs to find the most effective deterrent. "Off-Trail Hikers May Be Fined" worked best, but the rangers thought that was a little harsh. The most effective meadow preservative turned out to be simple social pressure. Visitors are more likely to wander off trail if they see others getting away with it. The presence of a uniformed ranger virtually eliminates stomping, which led one researcher to conclude, sadly, that most people knew they shouldn't meadow-stomp but did it anyway when nobody was looking. On jaunts through the meadow, I kept special watch over my infant cinquefoils. Anybody stomping them, I'd show 'em the wrath of der Wanderschuhe.

It's best to approach the Paradise meadows on a cool weekday when the morning mist conceals the valley and lifts like a succession of curtains. Wrap yourself in mittens, hats, and bundly jackets. You may feel overprepared in the parking lot, but I advise you to swallow hard and keep walking. I once frolicked like an idiot—shorts, huarache sandals, and a T-shirt—only to be caught in a July snowstorm that set my hands trembling and my feet dashing for the car. Bring a copy of Daniel Mathews's *Cascade-Olympic Natural History,* a delightful reference that includes histories of plant names, biographies of local botanists, and a recipe for nettle tea. Finally, walk alone. The key to a satisfying meadow day is the permission to stop, look, listen, and paw through the under-growth. This you alone can grant.

Starting low near the Paradise Inn one morning, I rambled through the meadow until the brush yielded to permanent snow. A short stroll from the inn brought me to a clump of green hellebore, which loves the swamps that pool here in early summer. The hellebore's massive leaves look gaudy in the meadow, home of the stubby and compact. It's easy to mistake the hellebore for skunk cabbage, which boasts similar elephantine leaves. Backcountry epicures take note: "Careless hikers thinking to enjoy a nice pot of boiled skunk cabbage," writes Harvey Manning, the Northwest's grandsire naturalist, "have mistakenly picked hellebore leaves instead and poisoned themselves; in one reported affliction, the victim's skin and eyeballs turn yellow and through his eyes the whole world looks yellow; in another, needle-like crystals from the plant's chemical constitution lodge in the throat and the patient dies." Hellebore's aliases—corn lily, Indian poke—raise no alarm in the mind of the unsuspecting gourmand. This seems unnecessarily sneaky. In the interest of fair play, hellebore deserves a new trail name: yelloweye, or old needlethroat.

Precedents exist. Until the arrival of European cuisine, Pacific Northwest Indians dined primarily on camas bulbs and salmon. Among the blue camas flowers often blooms the smaller white *Zigadenus venenosus*; the plants are easily mistaken for each other when they go to seed. One is camas. The other is death camas. Fair warning.

A brief stroll from the hellebore patch and a slight rise in elevation—maybe two hundred feet—brought me to a copse of high cedar and hemlock, trimmed with huckleberry, avalanche lily, and the ferocious pea of the hills: lupine. If there is a single flower that holds the secret of the mountain, it is the lupine. Texans call it the bluebonnet, which is a ridiculously dainty name for this mountain wolf (*lupulus*, Latin root for wolf) whose ability to survive is positively cockroachean. During the eruption of Mount St. Helens, the northern slope of the mountain was buried by an avalanche and incinerated by a pyroclastic flow of superheated gas, ash, and pumice. What was once a montane forest is now known as the Pumice Plain. On other parts of St. Helens vegetation reemerged from buried seeds and root fragments, but on the Pumice Plain nothing survived. Pioneering plants did blow in on the wind, though, and root in the rocky soil. Broadleaf lupine was among the first to arrive. Nearly twenty years after the eruption, it thrives and nurses other species by converting atmospheric nitrogen into soil-based nitrates and nitrites—turning air into fertilizer.

Lupine prefers meadows where its spokelike leaves can draw moisture from the air and channel it to the hub, where it rests as a perfect waterpearl. Sometimes the leaves hold their catch like peas static in the pod. This restraint produces in me the same delightful shiver evoked by rain on a window the moment before a gathering drop breaks the surface tension and sends a watercomet streaking south: the final moment of equilibrium. Rolling in the dewy meadow, I broke the spell and robbed the labor of a thousand leaves.

I walked farther up the meadow. A marmot eyed me from arm's length; I didn't see him until I'd passed and then whirled and jumped in that shock you get in a quiet house when somebody sneaks up and taps you. I yelped. The marmot didn't move. When my wits rejoined me, I sank my knees into an anemone patch and ran my fingers over its rich textures. In early summer the anemone resembles a tulip cup not yet open for business. The downy white fuzz on its stem captures drops of morning dew and traps the midday warmth by reflecting the sunlight. This is a sun-lover; the anemone blooms in the cool early summer and strains to maximize the faint heat of the meadow. The anemone's sepals act as a parabolic reflector, turning the flower cup into an inviting warming room for pollinating insects. On a clear day the anemone tracks the movement of the sun like a radar dish. Come August the plant goes to seed and assumes a new identity as the shaggy white seedhead that has inspired a delightful array of nick-names: Old Man of the Mountain, Mophead, Mouse on a Stick.

I love plant names. Mouse on a Stick. Paintbrush. Avalanche Lily. Beargrass. A good name joins imagination to cellulose and enhances a plant's chance of survival. It's easier to crush a field of plants than a stand of monkeyflower or partridgefoot. "Partridgefoot" implies a history, a family, a medicinal use. A proper name acknowledges the plant's value and implies that others have known it too. Somebody saw a seedhead and said, *Damn thing looks like a mouse on a stick.* "Mountain daisy" is an adequate name for the yellow-petaled *Erigeron peregrinum*, but its alias, "fleabane," recalls an age when medieval peasants relied on its supposed power to banish fleas from the home. "Heather" is lit-erally the heathen of the vegetable world. As heathen dwell outside the salvation of the church, so heather abides in the botanical wasteland.

Some names are poems of a single word; they bestow pleasure in the very act of speaking. Alumroot, with that languid *alum* sliding into the barrel-and-bang of *root*. Cinquefoil, which opens with the hard *sink* before melting into *foil*. Yellowdot saxifrage, in which the subtle explosion of *saxi* hides in the syllables like spice in an Indian curry. Salal, erotic *sss* coupled with the lascivious tongue-rise of *alal*, is the poet laureate of the Northwestern garden. The waxy shrub often appears in the poetry of Richard Hugo, who said salal was one of the few words he loved enough to own.

Other names beg for fanciful definitions. Hellebore, a soldier's war-whoop or a sleepy Dutch village. Broadleaf arnica and arrowleaf groundsel, meddling sisters in a parlor comedy. Latin names roll around the mouth like hard candy. Huckleberry: *Vaccinium deliciosum.* Vaccinium: "a name of great antiquity with no clear meaning." (It's so satisfying when botanists can't pin down the etymology of a common berry—reminds us that Clio still holds dear a few mysteries.) Deliciosum: of pleasant flavor. Pick a handful of the tart berries and crush them between your molars. Mmm. Mysteriously pleasant flavor.

Above the subalpine zone, about a mile out from Paradise, the growing season shrinks, the wind picks up, the soil turns nutrient-poor, and the firs shrivel until they turn into krummholz, a German word that means crooked wood. Height is a fickle quality on the mountain. At 5,000 feet trees that stand taller than the snowpack enjoy a year-round growing season. But above 7,000 feet, height becomes a handicap. Icy gusts shear the tops off trees sticking above the snowpack. The effect can be quite comic, as if a stout fir had gone in for a flattop. Survival this high requires horizontal growth. Hence the shrubby bodies— krummholz. On the mountain's eastern flank the whitebark pine, which can't abide the wetness of the west, thrives among the cedar, hemlock, and fir krummholz. Blasted and bleached, the trees look half skeleton, half flesh.

Like the marmot, the subalpine fir is finely tuned for high mountain survival. Its stubby upper branches grow close to the trunk to keep the fir from turning into a snow-laden kite in the high alpine winds. Heavy snow crushes its lowest branches into the ground, where they may take root and create a second or third tree; one fir can spawn an entire atoll. It may take a century for a fir to grow higher than the snowpack, but once it does it can photosynthesize all year round. The fifteen-foot snow base around Paradise leaves small trees dark and stunted most of the year. Those four-foot firs? They're sixty years old.

In late August the rot sets in. Like all mountain meadows, the Paradise valley is afflicted with a botanical form of Werner's syndrome; its plants age a month every week. When the radiant afternoons and deep lake skies begin to overstay their welcome, the omens of their leaving appear in the droop of leaves and decay of flowers. Lupine shed their flowers and shrivel into seedpods. Insects perforate hellebore leaves in perfect rectangles like computer punchcards. The metamorphosis of the anemone is long past; its sun-tracking sepals are halfway to mulch and its shaggy mane has been shagged by the wind. No longer mouse on a stick, it stands naked and stripped: stick.

I visited my revegetation plot and watched the greenhouse hatchlings shiver against the chill winds of September. At Paradise, like Summerland, autumn appears as a flash. One night I heard a report of a snow advisory in the Cascades, the first of the season. The next morning I drove to Paradise and saw the valley returned to whiteness. In a day the meadow died.

In November I returned to Paradise and nuzzled my car next to two other loners in the lot. A comfort of snow lay over the valley. Plywood covered the windows of the Paradise Inn. Hiking through the shin-deep powder was like wading through laundry detergent. The air carried the metallic tang of scentlessness. The snow had stripped all color away. At a low rise above the inn, I stopped and began digging for the meadow. I dug down five feet until specks of green clung to my mittens. There, beneath the white blanket, were the showy pigments of summer: three inches of green grass and pink heather buds no bigger than raspberry seeds. They waited, poised for the uprush of spring. Ready for the next season of life.

WE GO TO THE MOUNTAIN

Death became familiar during my time at the
mountain. Scott Fischer climbed up Everest
and never came down. A few months later
Lobsang Jangbu died in an avalanche on the same mountain. Two
Mount Rainier rangers were killed on a rescue mission high on the
Emmons Glacier. A week later two independent climbers died on the
same route. I attended more memorial services in one year than in
the previous thirty. But death was not, as Thomas Gray had written,
perpetually before my eyes. Nor could I dismiss it as the natural consequence of a risk-filled life. I found myself crossing its path at unexpected moments. One afternoon at a wedding reception I was overcome

by a rush of bittersweet sadness for Fischer, whom I had known only briefly. (Even *known* seems presumptuous; we'd talked.) It was the strangest pleasure, as if the joy and heartache created by his life passed over me like a warm breeze.

Mountains are as often a place of death as a source of life. In Yakama mythology the spirits of tribal ancestors watch over their children from the high Cascades. The Shoshones of Wyoming look upon the Tetons and see the resting place of ancients. Mountain burial places the dead closer to heaven so that their souls may find swift passage to the eternal sky. "Clutch the mountain" was the ancient Assyrian version of "kick the bucket." Mountains are especially associated with death in parts of Japan, where a coffin is known as a *yama oke*, mountain box, grave digging is *yama shigoto*, mountain work, and the funeral leader calls out *Yama yuki!* We go to the mountain! as the procession begins.

Some days people walk into Mount Rainier and vanish. A few years ago a woman parked her car at a picnic area and stepped into the trees. Her family believed she did not want to be found, and she never was. She joined at least fifty others whose bodies rest on the mountain, a population that makes Mount Rainier one of the world's most visible graveyards. If you walk into the ocean and drown, the tide will return your body to shore. If you walk into the mountains wishing to disappear, you will succeed. Animals and insects will pick your bones clean and glaciers will mill them to flour. To those seeking sanctuary, the mountain offers eternal refuge from civilization's billion-fingered reach. Scattering a loved one's ashes on Mount Rainier has become a common tribute to those who lived in the Northwest's rugged country. So many lives have been poured into the mountain's lakes, forests, and glaciers that Rainier stands as the region's greatest burial ground.

Not all those who go to the mountain rest easily. The bodies of at least a dozen fallen climbers remain sealed in glacial ice, as do the remains of thirty-two soldiers whose transport plane crashed into Mount Rainier shortly after the Second World War. During my time at the mountain I met a number of survivors of the recently deceased and the long passed, many of whom returned to Rainier year after year to revive the memory of those whom the mountain had taken. When we talked about the fatal events, I found most survivors willing, even eager, to tell me about the details. It was as if the narrative they'd honed over the months and years brought a small semblance of sense to their loved ones' passing.

In December 1946 a planeload of Marines bound for Seattle crashed into Mount Rainier, killing everyone aboard. Despite a massive recovery operation, all thirty-two men remain buried where they went down on the South Tahoma Glacier. Every summer since then, the families and friends of the victims gather at the mountain to mourn their lost boys. They rendezvous in late August behind the Ashford BP station in a field that the station owner calls a campground but that most folks would call a backyard. Relatives and friends of the dead Marines, most of them in their sixties, drive up in their RVs and stay for the weekend. They fly Marine Corps flags and sip diet soda in the awning shade, and on Saturday morning everybody gets dressed real nice and caravans to a spot overlooking the glacier. Somebody reads the ship's manifest and a squad of Fort Lewis Marines in dress blues fires a thirty-two-gun salute and the surviving mothers of the dead men weep.

Before one recent ceremony a group of grandfatherly ex-Marines directed me to Carolyn Pope, the sister of a lost Marine named Leslie Simmons, Jr. Her mother helped organize the early memorials in the fifties, and upon her passing Carolyn assumed responsibility for keeping the ceremony alive. "Have you seen any of the pictures?" she asked me. "Oh gosh, I've got plenty for you." She opened the trunk of her car and lifted out a leather scrapbook fat as a sack of grain. "Now here's where the plane hit," she said, pointing to a forty-nine-year-old Navy photograph of the South Tahoma Glacier. "And there's the rock-slide that came down on the plane." It was hard to tell the scale of things; I could make out the chute of the South Tahoma headwall and the rockpile at the bergschrund, where the wall meets the head of the glacier, but I couldn't say whether it was a few yards or a thousand feet high until—

Holy smoke. In the next photograph someone had circled the airplane. The rockfall's relation to the transport plane was approximately that of a book's spine to a period at the end of a sentence.

On the morning of Tuesday, December 10, 1946, thirty graduates of infantry training at the El Toro, California, Marine Air Station near San Diego boarded an R5-C transport plane bound for the Sand Point Naval Air Station in Seattle. The plane flew alongside five other troop planes ferrying fresh boots, as young Marines were called, up north. On board the second plane out of El Toro that morning was Leslie Simmons, Jr., Carolyn Pope's eighteen-year-old brother. Simmons had scored an extra week's furlough and was headed home for Christmas. His father had wired fifty dollars for a bus ticket, but Simmons spent the money on gifts and hitched a free ride on the transport. He had to borrow a suitcase to carry all the presents.

The flight was rough, noisy, and cold. The Marines watched ice form on the R5-C's wings. "We had everything in our sea bags on to try and keep warm," recalled Ron Coffey, a hometown friend of Simmons's from Kalama, Washington, who rode in a transport trailing Simmons's plane. The Marines didn't talk much. Most were airborne for the first time in their lives.

The six planes crossed the Washington border around four in the afternoon and flew into a storm that was unleashing the worst floods the state had seen since the Great Depression. Four pilots diverted their planes to Portland, but two came on to Seattle. Only one made it to Sand Point.

With darkness falling, pilot Robert Reilly, in the second transport, hailed the Civil Aeronautics Administration's Toledo, Washington, radio-range station for a routine checkover. Reilly told the Toledo station he was going to climb to 9,500 feet to get above the clouds icing up his wings. He signed off at four-thirteen in the afternoon. Minutes later, the twin-engine plane and its thirty-two passengers slammed into Mount Rainier at a speed of approximately one hundred ninety-five miles per hour. When a park ranger pulled Reilly's frozen body from the control column eight months later, the plane's altimeter was pegged at 10,300 feet.

"We kept up hope for quite a few weeks," recalled Carolyn Pope, who was then eleven-year-old Carolyn Simmons. "The fellow who taught Leslie to fly took my dad up to look for the plane. We all thought it had gone down around Mount St. Helens, which was good because Leslie had climbed that mountain; he could survive out there. They put in long hours flying around looking for that plane."

The official search shifted to Mount Rainier after park rangers reported hearing a plane fly over Longmire late that afternoon. Pilot Reilly had assumed he was directly over the Toledo station during his four-thirteen checkover. In fact, a seventy-mile-per-hour wind blowing in from the Pacific had pushed the airplane steadily east, and continued altering its course to head it straight for Rainier. But even if rescuers knew where the plane had gone down, there was little chance of reaching it in December. Blizzards pinned down searchers at Paradise and covered the wreckage in snow. Chief climbing ranger Bill Butler probed the Nisqually Glacier but found nothing. Dozens of frustrated searchers waited out the weather in Longmire. More than five feet of snow fell during the first three days of the search. If the plane was out there, it would stay buried until next summer's thaw.

The families of the missing men posted a five-thousand-dollar reward for the plane's discovery. Army, Navy, and Marine Corps pilots followed any lead they could find. Flyers from Sand Point Naval Air Station in Seattle took more than fifteen hundred photographs of the Cascades. Even private operators made reconnaissance runs. (It was on one such run, in fact, that Kenneth Arnold made the first infamous sighting of a "flying saucer" UFO.) Park rangers combed the lower mountain glaciers; military officials with gas-sniffing dogs and metal detectors joined the search. They found nothing.

Bill Butler went looking every chance he could, scouring the mountain's southern glaciers for any sign of the aircraft. On July 21, while climbing on his day off, Butler finally saw something. Looking through his field glasses from 11,000 feet on Success Cleaver, a ridge that runs parallel to the South Tahoma Glacier, Butler spotted a glint of metal on the ice. Looking closer, he made out the remnants of a bucket seat and a shard of plane wreckage. Excited as he was, it was too late in the day to cross the deep crevasses that lay between him and the plane. The next day Butler went up in a Navy plane to pinpoint the wreckage. Bruce Meyers, who worked that summer as a park naturalist and climbing ranger, directed a similar flyover a few weeks later. "You went up in a JRF, a twin-engine Grumman, which had a joehole in the bottom—opens like a hatch," Meyers recalled. "They put a harness on me, pushed me through, and said, 'You know where this thing is, direct us on over.' And I'd talk into the radio, 'A little right, little left.'"

Butler and a team of rangers, mountain guides, and Navy officers set up a base camp above Indian Henry's Hunting Ground. A park maintenance crew ran ten miles of telephone wire from Longmire to Indian Henry's to keep the salvage party in contact with authorities below.

On the morning of July 24 eight climbers, including Bill Butler, Bruce Meyers, and summit guide Dee Molenaar, started up the South Tahoma Glacier. The ice was so heavily crevassed that the team had to backtrack a number of times after facing impassable slots. Rock avalanches fell constantly, kicking up dust clouds so thick that Butler said it looked like fog. After eight hours of hard climbing the team discovered scraps of a Marine uniform, a Marine medical record, and bits of tail wreckage. Butler relayed a message to Longmire: The Marines were here.

The mountaineers found formers—the ribs of the aircraft—twisted and ripped apart by the shifting ice pack. Bruce Meyers and Dee Molenaar climbed fifty feet down a crevasse to find part of the tail section stuck in the frozen clutch. Wreckage was scattered over a quarter-mile area. But they found no bodies.

Butler and other rangers returned to the glacier over the next three weeks as the snow melted. Finally, on August 17, Butler, Meyers, and ranger Robert Weldon discovered the lost thirty-two. Butler spied the nose of the R5-C sticking out of the ice high near the headwall, where it had been hidden under the snow three weeks earlier. The rangers ascended the glacier to its birthplace, a harrowing course that only one summit party had ever attempted. The climb was nothing compared to the sight that awaited them at the bergschrund. Butler peered into the cockpit and beheld a scene of anatomical confusion. The force of impact was so great that the bodies of eleven Marines had been driven into a cockpit built for two.

"When we actually found the bodies it was eerie as hell, because they were all strapped in, right up the side of the aircraft," recalled Bruce Meyers. Snow and ice encased the nearest Marine to his chest. The next showed just to his neck. The next to his nose. The next to his eyes. "I still occasionally think about that," said Meyers. "Their bodies—those that we got out—were still in uniform. Nobody'd lost their arms or head or anything like that. They were still together. It was as if they'd gone to sleep."

There was no fire damage or trace of explosion. "When the aircraft went in, there had to be drift snow about fifty feet deep at the point of impact," said Meyers. "It just plowed in and stopped." The impact shattered the Marines' watches and broke most of their bones. There were no indications of suffering or struggle, nor signs that the pilot had pulled up at the last second. Everyone died in an instant.

Finding the bodies was one thing. Removing them was another. The Navy sent men from Sand Point, but with their smooth-soled shoes and canvas leggings the guides and rangers found them more hindrance than help. A team of Army mountain troops from Fort Collins, Colorado, had little better luck. The bergschrund of the South Tahoma Glacier, where the ice peels away from the 4,000-foot headwall, is one of the most dangerous spots on the mountain. Ice holding the cracked rock of the headwall together melts in late morning, sending a shower of boulders onto the glacier. Most arrive at killing speed.

"It was like an artillery barrage," said Bruce Meyers, a former Marine lieutenant. "As the rock came down the larger pieces broke up and turned into shrapnel. It was as close as you could come to an artillery barrage in civilian life.

"We had two people stationed on either side of the wreckage, about twenty yards apart, looking up all the time. One of them would yell, "*Rock!*" and we would dive in among the bodies. That's all we could do to save our lives."

Meyers and his colleagues were able to free the eleven Marines from the nose, but recovering the remaining twenty-one would require days of chipping the decomposing bodies out of the ice. The work was nightmarish. The salvage team could smell the corpses as they climbed the glacier. "The only way we identified the pilot was that this one skull had headphones on it," recalled Dee Molenaar. "It was like a crushed coconut."

The dead soldiers resembled the young climbers in many ways—age, rank, uniform—except one: The men in the plane had no eyes. The ordeal so unnerved one ranger that his supervisors sat with him all night to calm him down.

It quickly became apparent that the recovery of all the Marines could be accomplished only at the cost of the mountaineers' lives. Not even the corpses were safe. "We lined up eleven of the bodies on the

snow with the idea of putting them in body bags the next day,"
recalled Molenaar. "But during the night rocks fell down on them and
knocked one into a crevasse." At high camp on Success Cleaver, Lieutenant Colonel Warren Shelor, commander of the Army mountain
troops, considered his options. He could drop a demolition bomb on
the icefall above the wreck and bury the whole thing; he could cre-
mate the bodies with napalm; or he could leave and let nature take its
course. After consulting the parents at Longmire, Shelor and naval
authorities decided to leave the Marines with the mountain.

The rangers and mountain troops interred the eleven bodies in a
high crevasse, packed out a few personal effects, and left Leslie Simmons, Jr., and his thirty-one comrades to rest in the bosom of the
mountain.

The next day Park Superintendent John Preston issued a memo
declaring the South Tahoma Glacier closed to all travel. The ban
remains to this day.

I happened to be on the mountain the day two young men died, but I
didn't know it at the time. It was an August Sunday, one of the busiest
days of the year. So many tourists jammed Paradise that my father and
I spent twenty minutes trolling the parking lot for a free space and
waited in line to snap a picture at Glacier Vista. The mountain had
been reduced to the role of a photographer's backdrop. An East Indian
woman hiked in a brilliant orange sari. Bored teenagers sulked and
suffered the indignity of their parents' presence. A man whose
stomach embarrassed his shirt pushed a stroller up the trail. There was
no wilderness that day, no solitude, no contemplation, no peace.

A few hours before, the same mountain had taken the lives of Sean Ryan and Philip Otis. As we drove out of the park, I noticed the Longmire flag flying at half-staff.

"Wonder who died?" I said.

Sean Ryan and Phil Otis were probably the happiest men on the mountain that summer. The twenty-three-year-old Ryan had just graduated from the University of California at Santa Cruz. People described him as thin, but a photograph taken on the summit reveals the T-line of a climber's strong shoulders and back. Sometimes he wore his reddish hair in a ponytail and sometimes he wore it short and tousled. Other rangers never noticed the hoop clipped into his left lobe until an older climber referred to Ryan as "that hippie ranger with the earring." He had a slight New York accent and loved to listen to John Coltrane.

Ryan had spent the previous summer working at Glacier Basin as a park assistant with the Student Conservation Association (SCA), which provides the National Park Service with summer volunteers who work for fifty dollars a week plus housing. That taste of the ranger's life made him want more. At Santa Cruz the next winter he ran up his phone bill talking his way into a climbing ranger's job. Scott Wanek was the head climbing ranger at Rainier that summer. "The first day at the park, Sean and I talked about getting him into his housing and some other details," Wanek said. "We sat there looking at each other and Sean smiled like he couldn't believe this was really happening."

Phil Otis walked a step behind Sean Ryan. A year younger than Ryan, Otis was a senior at Bates College in Maine, where he'd developed an interest in a theologically grounded form of environmentalism. He'd petitioned the college to create his own "ecospirituality" major, and in his senior thesis used what he called the "positive nature-affirming resources" found in the Bible to propose a Christian theology that might heal the natural world.

Otis worked Ryan's old station as the SCA volunteer at Glacier Basin. He too had worked the phones that spring, calling day after day to talk his way into the job. He was a bubbly, outgoing kid whose favorite phrase was "I'm psyched!"

Sean Ryan spent most of June and July at Camp Schurman, the 9,700-foot-high camp that serves as a way station for climbers on their way up the Emmons Glacier. Otis camped below him at Glacier Basin, watching the meadow melt out and yield to glacier lilies, lupine, and deep green fescue. Deer slept nearby. During quiet moments, they wrote. "The sun is still shining off the snow on the summit," Ryan wrote to his parents, "whose glaciers will continue to feed the waterfalls and rivers that fill my water bottle and lull me to sleep each day." Otis wrote poems in his journal that connected the physical terrain of the mountain with inner passions and drives. "To be hard like black granite / or soft like a glacier's fresh fallen snow; to be fast like a waterfall / or slow like a lazy stream . . . " To read his words is to recognize the earnest innocence of a twenty-two-year-old kid meditating in the wilderness, wrestling with the problem of becoming a good and honorable man. "What better way to discover God," he wrote in his thesis, "than by sitting in quiet meditation above a cascading alpine waterfall?"

Their deaths began with a seemingly innocuous event. High on the Emmons Glacier on a Saturday afternoon, a climber stumbled and fell.

It was not a good week to fall. Earlier that month the freezing level had risen above 14,000 feet before settling back to 10,000 feet. Rain fell in the meantime, creating ten-foot icicles on the summit and lacquering the upper mountain with an inch of ice. "It's like you take a pitcher of water and pour it over the mountain, then let it freeze," explained Mike Gauthier, a climbing ranger and Ryan's partner that summer. Gauthier had noticed the tough conditions on a summit climb a few days earlier. "We stopped when we hit that ice and I told everybody, 'Nobody can fall here. There is no room for error.' If they'd fallen, I couldn't have stopped them."

So when John Craver, a forty-year-old California restaurateur who had climbed Rainier twice before, slipped on his way down from the summit, the glacier beneath him was steep and slick as a church gable. Instinctively, Craver's two rope partners threw themselves onto their ice axes, braking his fall and saving their own lives. In another two or three seconds, Craver could have pulled Anna Semansky and her father Michael to their deaths. They took stock: The Semanskys were fine, but Craver's ankle was broken. At 13,400 feet, on the largest glacier in the contiguous United States, John Craver couldn't walk.

Two climbers who witnessed Craver's fall helped move him and the Semanskys to a safer area alongside the bergschrund, where they stayed with Craver while the climbers trekked to Camp Muir, on the other side of the mountain, to find a ranger. At five o'clock they reached Muir, shouting, "We need a ranger!" They told rangers Jennifer Erxleben and George Beilstein that Craver was "shocky" and unequipped for an overnight bivouac.

Erxleben called the park's communications center near Ashford. District Ranger John Wilcox and Assistant Chief Ranger Bill Larson surveyed their options. The only helicopter able to reach 14,000 feet was a military Chinook, and scrambling a crew from Fort Lewis on a weekend would take at least four hours. By that time the eastern half of the mountain would be dark. But Wilcox and Larson did have troops in the high camps: Erxleben, Beilstein, and volunteer Dave Turner at Muir, and Sean Ryan at Camp Schurman.

At five-twenty the radio from Longmire to Camp Schurman, as often happens, went on the blink, but Wilcox and Larson were able to relay messages to Ryan through another ranger station. By five-thirty-five they knew that Ryan, Seattle Mountain Rescue volunteer Luke Reinsma, and SCA volunteer Phil Otis were up there.

It wasn't a veteran crew. Erxleben and Ryan were first-year climbing rangers, although both had a number of summits under their belts. Otis had done some rock climbing, but his Cascade experience was limited: once up Mount Baker, once up Mount Rainier. Reinsma, a forty-seven-year-old English professor, hadn't climbed Rainier since his first summit seven years earlier and was still recovering from a bout of double pneumonia. The park's most experienced climbers were off duty. Wilcox and Larson scoured the mountain for support. Rainier Mountaineering had a full contingent of clients at Camp Muir, but RMI president Lou Whittaker offered to send a couple of guides up from Paradise to handle the park radio at Muir.

At six Wilcox and Larson set a plan into motion. Ryan, Otis, and Reinsma would climb up from Camp Schurman to Craver with splints and bivouac gear, stabilize him, and spend the night with him and the Semanskys. Erxleben, Beilstein, and Turner would leave Muir after midnight carrying heavy evacuation gear; they'd reach the party around six the next morning and either lower Craver down to Camp Schurman or assist with a daytime helicopter pickup.

Ryan, Otis, and Reinsma chowed down. They'd need plenty of fuel for the climb. Reinsma warmed a can of beef stew while Otis spread peanut butter and jelly across a flour tortilla. Phil Otis was psyched. He'd talked late into the previous night about climbing routes and crevasse rescues. Now he'd not only climb with Ryan, but assist on an SAR (Search and Rescue) to boot. He couldn't believe his luck.

With his supervisor out of town, Otis had played hooky Saturday afternoon to climb with Ryan to Schurman. Ryan had covered for his friend by pretending Otis was hiking up from Glacier Basin at the end of his shift, when in fact he was standing beside him; this led to some initial confusion among Wilcox and Larson at the communications center. When a radio call came in, Otis asked Reinsma to answer. "I'm not supposed to be here," he said.

Sean Ryan was no less excited. "This is it," he said as the three of them sorted their gear. "This is what we've been training for. This is the big time!"

Luke Reinsma didn't share their youthful ardor. Nearly thirty years Otis and Ryan's senior, Reinsma wasn't sure he could huff a full pack to the bergschrund. *I'm not half as strong as these guys,* he thought. But he knew how to take care of a broken ankle, and Ryan and Otis didn't. So he went. He assumed both Ryan and Otis were well-trained, experienced climbers. They assumed the same of Reinsma. All three were wrong.

Their sixty-pound loads would have capsized a mule. Each carried two sleeping bags, two sleeping mats, one tent, food, and fuel. In addition, Ryan's pack held two pulleys, a prusik cord, a figure eight, webbing, a first aid kit, four carabiners, three bivvy sacks, a SAM splint, an Ace bandage, a bottle of Advil, a stove, a picket, a water bottle, a

Thermarest pad, sunscreen, a 4.5-volt battery, sunglasses, fleece gloves, a down jacket, and a cookpot.

At seven o'clock Ryan, Otis, and Reinsma started up the glacier. The sun was still high, but the temperature was beginning to drop and the wind blew cold enough to numb skin. John Craver sat alone at the bergschrund blowing a whistle.

Worried that they wouldn't survive the night, the Semanskys had left Craver with extra clothing, food, and water late that afternoon and climbed down to Camp Muir. They told Jennifer Erxleben that their companion was warm and comfortable. He had some Advil and Percodan, but didn't want to take the latter for fear of slowing his heart. The Semanskys detailed Craver's location and said he'd be signaling on his whistle every five minutes.

The Schurman team made slow progress. "It was a step and a breath even at the outset," recalled Luke Reinsma. Even at a moderate pace, Ryan and Otis were too fast for the mountain rescue volunteer. The rope stretched taut between Otis and Reinsma. "It was as if they were trying to pull me, faster, up the mountain," he said.

A few minutes out of camp, Ryan realized he'd forgotten snow wands to mark the trail. He called back to Reinsma, wondering if the team should go back for them. *He's asking me?* thought Reinsma. They continued without the wands.

Reinsma apologized for dragging. "That's okay!" Otis shouted back. "We need you!" Reinsma took two breaths for every step.

Less than an hour out of camp, Ryan called in to ranger Ben Olver at the White River station, looking for advice. "This mountain rescue guy's slowing us down," he said. Olver advised against dropping

Reinsma; no matter how slow they were going, three climbers were safer than two.

Altitude-induced nausea began to compound Reinsma's fatigue, and by eight-thirty he was spent. He motioned for a break. The team huddled to hear themselves over the wind. Olver relayed the news to Ryan that the Semanskys had climbed down to Muir, which angered Phil Otis, who couldn't believe anyone would abandon an injured partner. The new development meant Ryan's team was carrying three times more equipment than was needed, giving Ryan and Reinsma a face-saving option. Reinsma offered to unclip and pack the extra bags back to Schurman, lightening Ryan and Otis's load and freeing them from the burden of his slowness. Ryan agreed.

Reinsma turned back for Camp Schurman alone. A blanket of clouds spread over the Cascades below him. The setting sun sprayed crimson across the horizon. Ryan and Otis continued up the mountain, so slowly, Reinsma thought when he turned to watch them go, that it seemed they hardly moved at all. They climbed under a clear sky and a moon so bright they didn't need headlamps.

Two hours later the mountain's attitude had changed. At eleven-twenty Ben Olver radioed Ryan for a status check. "We're at 12,900," Ryan told him, audibly gasping. The wind howled through the radio. "It's slow going," he said. They were having equipment trouble. "We lost a crampon," Ryan said. "It blew away." Luke Reinsma, listening in on the Camp Schurman radio, cringed. He remembered seeing Phil Otis strap his crampons tight with duct tape before they set out. At the time he thought it a smart precaution. In fact Otis's hinged Salewas were sized too big for his boot; only the tape held them on. On a summit climb the previous month he'd stepped clean out of his spikes. Now at 12,900 he'd lost the entire left frontpiece.

They made progress despite Otis's equipment problems. Ryan said he could see the bergschrund up ahead. Olver told them to take it easy and have a good climb. Ryan signed off with his park identification number: "6-4-8."

Sometime before midnight Jennifer Erxleben, George Beilstein, and Dave Turner rose from a restless sleep in the Butler Hut at Camp Muir and roped up on the Cowlitz Glacier. Ben Olver attempted to raise Sean Ryan on the radio. "648, White River," he said. No answer. "648, White River." Nothing. Ken Davies, a ranger on road patrol, stopped along State Highway 410 and scanned the Emmons Glacier for signs of headlamps. He saw none.

Sometime before midnight, Sean Ryan and Phil Otis stopped climbing. What happened next is conjecture. Otis may have planted his ice axe and released it momentarily, perhaps to adjust a crampon. On a freezing, windy night Ryan's hands were bare, suggesting that he removed his fleece gloves to retrieve his radio from the top pocket of his pack, which was unzipped. "You'll often reach back for something like that if you're in the middle of a climb and don't want to take your pack off," a ranger told me. One or both of them fell. It makes little difference who went first, because in an instant both were hurtling down the ice and gaining momentum at something less than thirty-two feet per second per second.

They fought it. Their scrape marks began at 13,200 feet, a three-foot-wide track scarred by half-inch grooves, and ended at the top of an ice cliff at 12,200 feet, which is like sliding down the Chrysler Building. At the ice cliff they shot into the air and fell two hundred feet more before coming to rest on the Winthrop Glacier, their rope coiled into a horseshoe between them.

Sometime before midnight, moments before they fell, John Craver sat two hundred vertical feet above Sean Ryan and Phil Otis, blowing a whistle.

Ben Olver radioed Sean Ryan for the next six hours. He received no reply. At Camp Schurman, Luke Reinsma decided to give it another try. He packed a smoke grenade to signal the helicopter, and a pair of crampons for Phil Otis, and roped into an independent climbing team led by Ian Williams. But again sickness overcame him. Reinsma dropped out at four a.m. and returned to Schurman alone. An hour later Ian Williams discovered the frontpiece of Phil Otis's crampon lying on the snow. He pocketed it and kept climbing. He found Otis's ice axe planted upright along the trail and noticed some disturbing scratches immediately downslope. He bagged the axe and kept climbing. When he reached the bergschrund, he told Jennifer Erxleben what he had found.

Erxleben had reached John Craver around seven Sunday morning. Except for the broken ankle, he was stable and upbeat. Now the search turned to Ryan and Otis.

Erxleben called Ben Olver at White River, where Mike Gauthier had recently come on duty. When she mentioned the ice axe, Gauthier cut in and described the extra axe kept at Camp Schurman. Was it blue with red webbing? Yes, it was, Erxleben said. Gauthier described Phil Otis's crampon to Erxleben. She held the exact frontpiece in her hand.

"That pretty much said it all," recalled Gauthier. He and Olver loaded their climbing gear into a Park Service truck and drove to the Kautz Creek helipad to meet the Chinook. The drive around Highway 123 usually takes eighty minutes. Gauthier made it in forty.

At nine-thirty Sunday morning Scott Wanek, Ken Davies, and climbing rangers John Gillett and Ross Freeman boarded a military CH-46D Chinook and flew to Craver's bivouac site. The rangers loaded Craver aboard and hunkered down against the snowstorm blown up by the chopper blades. Forty minutes later, eighteen hours after his accident, John Craver was lifted out of the helicopter at the Kautz Creek landing pad and loaded into an ambulance. Now Gauthier, Olver, and ranger Rick Kirschner hopped in the chopper and joined the search.

The flight to the Emmons took only a few minutes. The chopper passed over Paradise, already filling with tourists, and rose to the top of the Emmons Glacier, gleaming slick in the midmorning sun. The helicopter swept down the ice. While Gauthier and Kirschner scanned the lower Emmons, Davies looked upglacier and spotted the missing team lying among broken blocks of ice. The chopper moved in close enough for the rangers to recognize Sean Ryan's green National Park Service jacket. The sun winked off his gold NPS badge.

While the pilot hovered the Chinook, Kirschner and Gauthier hopped onto the snow. Gauthier ran to Ryan, his best friend and climbing partner. "I knew he was dead," Gauthier said. "I'd seen bodies on glaciers." Snow had drifted over their bodies and faces. Their hair was frozen. As Gauthier lifted Ryan's head, he felt for an instant as if he might pull the entire scalp clean of the skull. There were few bruises and none of the blackfreeze marks of frostbite. "It was Sean,"

Gauthier said. "I was afraid of what I might find, but it was just . . . Sean."

Sometime after noon Sunday, a ranger lowered the flag at Longmire to half-staff.

Ryan and Otis's death shook Gauthier more than anyone at the mountain. The moment he saw Ryan's body he swore off climbing forever, wanted to leave his gear on the glacier. A few months later the mania reversed. "I felt invincible when I climbed," he told me. "I could not fall." For the next year he wore Sean Ryan's size 10½ hiking boots. He climbed through tears with Phil Otis's girlfriend to spread Otis's ashes on the summit. "I feel like much of my life has been defined by this incident," Gauthier said, a year after it occurred.

In Gauthier I found one of the mountain's most unusual specimens, a climber who wrestled with the intellectual implications and emotional trauma of his job even as he relished performing it. He was only twenty-six the summer Ryan and Otis died, but had worked on the mountain most of his adult life. I first encountered him at the public memorial service for Ryan and Otis. He read a poem by Ursula K. Le Guin, which struck me as odd. Eulogists at climbing funerals usually turn to John Muir or Wendell Berry; Le Guin was best known for her science fiction. And yet her poem fit perfectly. *Need to meet this guy*, I thought.

Some evenings I'd stop by his bunkhouse behind the White River station and share a burrito-and-Coke dinner and we'd talk about books and mountains and politics and our hopelessly disarrayed love lives. He was usually grimy from a three-day shift at Camp Schurman, and clomped around in unlaced climbing boots, white longjohns, and sweat-matted hair. We ate on a table decorated with dirty plates, old newspapers, a copy of the *Norton Anthology of Modern Poetry*, and a volume of Neruda. A cylinder of Gatorade mix sat next to bottles of Knob Creek whiskey and Kahlua on the counter. He ate chocolate frosting out of the can, whistled like a marmot, and every once in a while drove into Seattle to drop a hundred bucks on sushi. Most everyone called him Gator because his fourth-grade football coach in Olalla, Washington, had looked at "Gauthier" on his helmet and said *I can't pronounce that damn name*, and since the kid wore a "Ragin' Cajun" jersey to practice and "Gauthier" kind of looked like "Gator," he became Gator. He uses it so much some people don't know his first name is Mike.

He said what he thought and he thought a lot. He had no patience for the budget politics and bureaucratic doublespeak that the Park Service, like all government agencies, tends to foster. His willingness to speak out made his superiors nervous. It drew me to him like a moth.

Gator spent a lot of nights alone on the mountain, though he never wanted for company when he desired it. His job involved a certain amount of public relations, at which he excelled. He made trail conversation with pot-smoking climbing bums as easily as he chatted up narc-squad cops. He'd talk about anything, anytime. Once he told me, in all seriousness, that he was considering a run for governor in 2004. "I figure I'll be ready by then," he said. Climbers looked on him with awe, told him he was living their dream. "People tell me, 'Oh man, you have the best job in the world, I'd do anything to trade for your job.' And I say, 'Great, what do you do?' And they tell me and I say, 'Let's trade for a year, I need to make some *money*.' One guy, he thought I could walk on water because I climbed glaciers—and in a sense I guess I could—but I mean, man, he just thought that was the *shit*, climbing Mount Rainier all those times [eighty at last count] and going through all the accidents and the rescues and the storms and the craziness and the niceness and the fun. The mountain attracts ten thousand people a year to test their mettle. For some people it's good, for some people it's a catharsis, and for some people it costs them. And when it costs them, it's hard."

He'd seen some bad craziness on Rainier. "I've seen people in thongs up on the glaciers. *High*—I mean we're talking thongs at ten thousand feet, dress shoes at twelve-five. One guy came up to camp. Classic bonehead. Showed up with his shirt off, a pair of shorts, combat boots, and a knife. He goes, 'I know what you have to tell me because you're rangers and all, but come on. Give me the real scoop. What is the bare minimum a *real man* needs to climb Mount Rainier?' I wanted to look at him and say, 'You look man enough to do it the way you are. *Hit the trail, buddy!*'"

It wasn't easy to track Gator down; his work took him up to the summit one day, across the mountain the next. But his stories were worth my efforts. One afternoon I caught him at White River and he told me about four climbers he'd passed on the Inter Glacier trail. They were trudging up the glacier with a rope strung around their necks like a four-knotted noose. Gator laughed, but if one of those climbers slipped, he'd have to risk his life to save them. "It's frustrating because people are allowed to do whatever they want on the mountain," he said. "I'm all for letting people go out and test their own abilities, but when they hurt themselves it affects other people around them. And that's what's hard. I try not to be the one to tell people,

'Don't do that.' I could've yelled down, *Hey, you guys gotta rope up!* but I thought, Nope. They're adults."

It took a year for Gator to come to terms with his grief, and then in his off-duty hours he began rock climbing at Vantage and Leavenworth. He booked an ambitious itinerary during his four-month winter furlough: rock climbing at Joshua Tree National Park; technical rescue training in Sedona, Arizona; ice climbing in Valdez, Alaska; ice climbing in Pennsylvania, New Hampshire, Vermont, and upstate New York. A few days before he left, I stopped by and he showed me the down climbing suit he'd ordered for the winter's ultimate adventure, an expedition into the Alaska Range to scale some unclimbed peaks and new routes on mountains northeast of Mount McKinley. He was excited; I was a little spooked. His itinerary reminded me of another climber and the choices he'd made.

"Be careful," I told him as I left.

I don't know if he heard me.

Shortly after the Marines were found in the summer of 1947, one of the bereaved mothers, Mrs. Rolland Tisch, wishing to calm the fears of the other parents whose children would never rest in parish cemeteries, wrote a letter to each of them. She described Mount Rainier as a headstone created by the hand of God. How much better that their son find peace there, she wrote, than to lay him "in a small plot of earth in some cemetery and erect a headstone above it, made by the puny hands of man, when already he has a resting place provided for him that man, with all his skill, ingenuity and money, could never equal in magnificence and grandeur."

Standing before the mountain in all its magnificence at Sean and Phil's memorial, however, I couldn't shake the sense that it remained cold ice and rock. Puny though our hands may be, they're all the comfort we possess. When Sean Ryan's body was sent to his parents in New York, the men in his family gathered to build by hand the *yama oke* in which he was cremated. A year later they came West to return his body to the mountain and grasp the hands of those loved by their son.

On the summit and in the glaciers they wait, Sean and Phil and the thirty-two Marines. They wait for the rest of us to come to the mountain.

THE CONSTANT
PRESENCE OF GOD

O n a late summer afternoon choked with mosquitoes and yellow jackets, some friends and I hiked to Tolmie Peak, a few miles northwest of the Carbon Glacier. The heat, usually so rare on Rainier, bore down on us with a relentlessness surpassed only by that of the bugs. Perspiration and insect repellent trickled down our noses and numbed our lips. We stopped every mile to douse our heads. At last we reached Eunice Lake, a deep snowmelt pool at the foot of a high mountain cirque, which should have provided a refreshing reward for our labors. Instead we pressed on. Tolmie Peak Lookout, a cabin that looked the size of a Monopoly house from the lake, remained another half-hour away at the top of the cirque. Why did we have to reach it? Why go to the top? Swatting bugs and grumbling up the switchbacks, my mind rummaged through the possibilities and eliminated every answer but one, which came to me from a childhood Sunday school lesson on the Temptation of Christ. "Taking him to a very high mountain, the devil showed him all the kingdoms of the world and their splendor. 'I will give you all these,' he said, 'if you will fall at my feet and worship me.'"

We want to see what God and the devil see.

Every now and then the mountain beckons the spiritually enfervored who want to walk to the summit to see God. They usually don't make it very far, but once in a great while the rangers or RMI guides have to talk a Jesus freak out of the summit crater caves. I've never fathomed why we, like the psalmist, look to the hills for our salvation. If God exists in all things, it makes as much sense to look in the ditches and drainfields. Does God exist to different degrees in things, more in mountains than in the sea? This seems too slippery a slope; there lie ecclesiastical councils on the gradations of God inherent in the treasures and trash of the Earth. Pascal once defined nature as an infinite sphere, whose center is everywhere and circumference nowhere. I find this a satisfactory atlas of God's whereabouts. But I'm still left puzzling over our innate tendency to seek God in the hills.

I took the question to Father Timothy Sauer, whom I'd heard speak at a memorial service for Ryan and Otis. Father Sauer serves as campus minister for O'Dea High School, a Catholic institution on Seattle's First Hill. He fits the role of Catholic boys' school priest the way John Wayne slipped into a ten-gallon hat. With black Vince Lombardi–era glasses and a monkish haircut, Sauer conveys the impression that he's been trading in discipline his entire life.

"When I'm in the mountains I sense the solitude, the majesty," Sauer said. "For me there's a powerful awareness of God's presence." Sauer had worked between seminary semesters as a seasonal ranger at Rainier, and stayed as close to the mountains as he could. His office wall was covered by a floor-to-ceiling poster of a larch forest turning autumn gold in the Swiss Alps. "Even when it's wreathed in clouds, you know Mount Rainier is there," he said. "It's an ever-present reality. It's a symbol of the constant presence of God."

Willi Unsoeld, the legendary Pacific Northwest climber who died in an avalanche on Rainier, once said people don't climb mountains because they're there; people climb because they yearn for convergence. "When you stand on Mount Rainier," Sauer said, "you look in a circle, and valleys and glaciers and rivers and ridges radiate like the spokes of a wheel. You're standing on the point of union, the place where everything comes together."

So many sacred mountains rise from the Earth that it's rare to find a culture that doesn't venerate some peak, point, crest, or hill. In Nepal the mountain the rest of the world calls Everest is known as Chomolungma, mother goddess of the Earth. Thousands of Hindu pilgrims each year circumnavigate the Tibetan peak Kailas, upon whose summit dwells Shiva, Lord of the World. Buddhists and Jainists also hold Kailas sacred. The list goes on. The Buddha is said to have first perceived and understood the dharma upon India's Peak of the Vultures. Zeus, supreme god of the ancient Greeks, ruled from high on Mount Olympus. Muhammad met the angel Gabriel and received the word of God in a cave on Mount Hira. Every year 300,000 Shinto faithful make the arduous ascent of Fuji-san, Japan's honorable Mount Fuji. And, of course, Moses received the Ten Commandments on Mount Sinai.

It's the same image the world over: the mountain as the link between heaven and earth, the point of intersection between the mortal and eternal spheres. Not long after they scooped up mud from the Tigris and Euphrates river deltas and invented dried brick, Sumerian architects began stacking their ingenious blocks together to form temples. Their typical form, wrote Joseph Campbell, "was that of the ziggurat in its earliest stages—a little height, artificially constructed, with a sanctuary on its summit for the ritual of the world-generating union of the earth-goddess with the lord of the sky." The Assyrians and Babylonians, who perfected the ziggurat, made the mountain-temple connection more explicit. Sacred Babylonian temples were called "Mount of the House," "House of the Mountain of All the Lands," and "Mount of Storms." The very word is derived from the Assyrian *zigguratu*, summit. As soon as humans devised bricks with which to build them we constructed mountains on which to worship our gods.

The funny thing is, when you're actually *on* a mountain, I mean up high where the air's thin, reverence and worship are quite the last things on your mind. You're worried about snow gumming up your crampons, the sun cracking your lips, your water freezing, those clouds moving in from the Sound, whether you packed enough food, and whether to turn back before the weather deteriorates any further. After talking with Father Sauer, I went through a brief spirit-of-the-hills phase during which I packed theological tracts next to the freeze-dried chili whenever I went to the mountain. The books provided good reading on nights I stayed low, but when I climbed to Camp Muir I'd inevitably pull the two-pound Jerusalem Bible out of The Renegade and wonder, *Now what the hell's this for?*

There's some of this ambivalence in the Bible itself. The New Testament abounds with mountains as symbols of grandeur and relief, but Old Testament mountains tend to be forbidden and forbidding. Christ was forever trudging up and down the Holy Land's humble peaks: to give the Sermon on the Mount, to pray at the Mount of Olives, to appear resurrected on Mount Tabor. Mountains were Christ's sanctuary; after a hard day he often "went up to the mountain to pray" (Mark 6:46) or "withdrew again to the mountain" (John 6:15). I haven't been to Israel, but I've seen pictures. Those are Southern California mountains: low scrubby hills whose visitors stand in danger only of catching a light breeze. I prefer the Old Testament mountains. They're not physically grander, but they convey a greater sense of the actual foreboding you feel on glaciered peaks. The Tower of Babel provoked God's wrath by reaching too close to heaven. Everyone knows God passed the Ten Commandments to Moses on Mount Sinai, but that mountain's unwelcoming and ominous climate is much less publicized. The consequences for any Israelite who scaled Sinai before God had finished his business with Moses were tremendous: "Whoever touches the mountain will be put to death. No one must lay a hand on him: he must be stoned or shot down by arrow, whether man or beast; he must not remain alive." Old Testament mountains did not beckon the timid.

Maybe I'm thinking too literally. Perhaps I'm expecting mountains to turn climbers into Baptist missionaries when that's not the point at all. It's not that high places point you directly toward conversion. It's that these places induce in the visitor the sort of awe and trepidation that lies at the heart of the spiritual self. There's an element of religion that can't be taught or told; it has to be felt. Theologian Rudolf Otto described the feeling as something that "may burst in sudden eruption up from the depths of the soul with spasms and convulsions, or lead to the strangest excitements, to intoxicated frenzy, to transport, and to ecstasy." It may just as easily arrive as a hushed, trembling, and speechless humility. This *mysterium tremendum,* as Otto described it, is the experience of finding oneself in the overwhelming presence of the holy.

The power of the holy to rattle the boots of the soul is uncannily similar to the wonderment of the senses aroused by the great mountains of the world: trepidation, awe, tremendousness, mystery—all familiar companions of the mountain traveler. All elements, too, of the sublime. A century and a half before Otto, the English essayist Edmund Burke described a similar encounter with the sacred in *A Philosophical Enquiry into the Origin of Our Ideas of the Sublime and Beautiful.* Burke's vision involved a trembling, reverent awe in the face of power, darkness, vastness, and terror, with an emphasis on the last. "Whatever is fitted in any sort to excite the ideas of pain and danger . . . or operates in a manner analogous to terror, is a source of the sublime," he wrote. This moment of exquisite terror is "the strongest emotion which the mind is capable of feeling."

That mountains would become the primary destination for those in search of the sublime would have come as no surprise to the English writers who preceded Burke. Seventeenth-century poets looked to the hills and saw fear, fright, alarm, and destruction. By the time Burke declared terror a desirable good, the mountains were well established as a great storehouse of the stuff. A peek at the day's best-sellers yields a litany of epithets against the hills. In his first *Anniversary Poem* of 1611, John Donne includes mountains among the major symptoms of a world whose beauty "is decayd, or gone." For Donne the shining hills were nothing but "warts, and pock-holes in the face of th'earth." In his diary of 1646 the English traveler John Evelyn described his passage through the "strange, horrid, and fearful crags and tracts" of the Alps, which he thought embarrassed the even plains of Europe, "as if Nature had here swept up the rubbish of the earth."

"Mountains were 'unjust,' 'hook-shoulder'd,' they were deformities of the earth; their peaks frightened the heavens," wrote Marjorie Hope Nicolson in *Mountain Gloom and Mountain Glory*. "They were excrescences, swellings, protuberances, which by their monstrous weight threatened the balance of the earth." Their shifting clouds and sudden storms, cracking ice and crashing rockfall attracted the darker monsters of the imagination. Though science may explain away the mysterious forces of wind, weather, and gravity, high on Rainier when you feel yourself in play among those shifting elements, you may, if you seek it, catch the fading scent of the sublime.

A friend and I drove into the North Cascades on a late October afternoon when the vine maples had bled all over the hillsides and the subalpine firs wore a coat of early sugar. As we slowed to pass through a mountain town's speed trap, the valley around us opened to reveal not the jagged peaks that we knew stood there, but a shifting battlement of mist as eerie and ominous as dry ice in a Halloween punch. A roiling airborne sea. Corpse-grey and moist, the spooky wrap washed over the hills now thick and airplane-swallowing, now thin as a dry cough. The hair on my neck sprang to life and I had no doubt that we were rising into the realm of the sacred.

It's in these mysterious moments that we most feel the fearful presence of the holy. In the swirling ambiguity of clouds, all worldly bearings are lost. "When we know the full extent of any danger," Burke wrote, "when we can accustom our eyes to it, a great deal of the apprehension vanishes." I'm reminded of moments in the mist of St. Andrew's Park, or in a whiteout on the Muir snowfield, when the world was reduced to Descartes's maxim. I think, I am, but the world beyond me remains in doubt.

This is what we see when we look up at Rainier: the beauty, the horror, the awe, the unbelievability of size that confirms our own inconsequence on this Earth. We look at the mountain, like God, and can imagine nothing larger. Its incomprehensible lifespan reminds us of the fleeting mortality of our own bones. It looms over our lives on clear days and stays present but hidden through the clouds of winter. Like God it remains everywhere forever.

NAUGHT WITHOUT
PRUDENCE

e're supposed to hate quitters. From an early age we're trained to persevere, carry on, never surrender. "A quitter never wins and a winner never quits" is one of the first bromides to poison a child's mind. The depths of our abhorrence are illustrated by our sparing use of the noun. It's a severe last resort, used after weakling, crybaby, and loser have been hurled to no effect. *Quitter!* is such a harsh reproach that more than one angry leave-taker has spun heel and rejoined the game, his technique ablaze with the fury of I'll-show-you.

Me, I love to quit. Where some see an act of cowardice, I see a redirection of energy. I quit Mr. Chun's baseball team in ninth grade and won a summer of lazy play. I quit my job on a Wall Street trade magazine—which required me to phone investment bankers, accept verbal abuse, and print outrageous conjectures and lies about upcoming stock issues—and gained a more meaningful existence. Few moments in life are as thrilling as those following a notice-posting. I have friends who experience something close to amphetamine rushes after they quit their jobs. The freedom from rote chores and dumb bosses compels them to publicize their newfound gaiety and ask their friends why they didn't do this sooner. Some have considered taking a new job just to renew the exhilaration of quitting.

There are honorable and dishonorable forms of the quit. The mountain has taught me the honorable. Implicit in the honorable quit is the knowledge of one's limits, and the confidence to live within them—or at least know when, and when not, to push. I once met my limit, quite literally, near the summit of Mount Ruth. I was on my way to Camp Schurman, the 9,500-foot-high climbing camp at the junction of the Emmons and Winthrop Glaciers. The park's seasonal rangers were holding their annual Schurman spaghetti feed, and Gator had invited me to join the party. When I checked in at the White River station, though, Gator was at Kautz Creek, on the other side of the mountain, helping load a new solar toilet into an army helicopter. The double-rotored Huey would drop the toilet off at Camp Schurman, and the rangers were hoping to pack some party supplies along for the ride.

I hung around the office waiting for him to call in. The White River station is a cozy log house with a public living room complete with green leather couch and a propane fireplace, connected to a small warren of cubicles. I dipped in and out of a book that couldn't hold my attention, read the safety-first posters on the walls, and glanced at a plaque dedicated to Phil Otis and Sean Ryan. A quote from the nine-teenth-century mountaineer Edward Whymper hung nearby:

> *Climb if you will but remember, that courage and strength are naught without prudence, and that a momentary negligence may destroy the happiness of a lifetime. Do nothing in haste, look well to each step and from the beginning think what may be the end.*

Day hikers drifted in to ask about trail conditions and campground vacancies, and ranger Ben Olver did his best to answer their questions and fill the dull stretches in between. He and Pam Cox, a backcountry ranger, absently chatted about climbing later in the week.

"Hope it's not icy," said Ben.

"Oh, I don't climb in ice," Cox replied. "Glacial ice is one thing, but when it ices over..."

"Last year's climb the day after the spaghetti feed, it was very icy. Have you seen the pictures?"

"Just the one of Gator," Cox said. The picture, tacked above the dresser in Gator's room, showed him standing next to a curtain of ici-cles on the summit.

Gator called in and told Olver he was still loading the Huey, which they weren't sure would fly that day because the mountain was so socked in. Rain drizzled outside the window of the White River sta-tion. Olver handed the phone to me. "Why don't I meet you up there?" Gator said. "Ben knows the route. He'll show it to you."

Ben traced a dogleg from Glacier Basin up the Mount Ruth ridge over to Camp Curtis and up to Camp Schurman. "Take a left about a hundred yards out of Glacier Basin, cross the Inter Fork River, and head up to the top of the ridge," he told me. "You'll find the trail eventually, and just follow the ridgeline on up."

The wide promenade that leads to Glacier Basin was cut more than eighty years ago by the Mount Rainier Mining Company, which pursued silver and copper claims here from 1914 to 1930. The trail is actually the old Starbo Mine road, which follows the Inter Fork of the White River up to the Basin meadow, where miners once spent summers digging through pumice. The site of the current campground once bustled with a hotel and a power plant. Although the company worked the area for sixteen years, little silver or copper was shipped downmountain. Abandoned tonnage rests along the trail—twisted cable, big scoop buckets, the wheel of an aerial tramway.

I passed two climbers on the trail to Glacier Basin. Their plastic climbing boots squeaked. Metal snow anchors called "deadmen" stuck out of their packs. "How's it up high?" I asked.

"Windier'n a hoot," said one. "Ripped our tent up. Made it a short trip."

They continued down and I looked up at the mountain through clearing skies. The glaciers were clear, the summit placid.

At Glacier Basin I shared a lunch table with a marmot, then turned ridgeward. Up a dune of gravel-size pumice, past gnarled stands of cedar, subalpine fir, and mountain hemlock krummholz. Clumps of tiny mountain daisy and dwarf lupine huddled together, making their own soil by composting last year's yield and trapping grains of airborne and waterborne rock. In the forest two hours behind me, the lupine matched the diameter of a coffee mug. Now it was smaller than Roosevelt's head on a dime.

A rainstorm the previous day had wiped out most footprints, but I found the faint outline of a trail and began following a set of fresh soles. To my left and down five hundred feet of airshaft lay the Emmons Glacier, the largest body of moving ice in the contiguous United States, striped like a tiger by the summer's windblown grit. The prints led me up a ridge skirting a snowfield that, I later learned, had been scarred with stairsteps and a traverse until rain washed them away. The higher I went the more intimate became my bond with the prints that led me. I adopted their creator as an imaginary trailmate, measured their size against mine (size 10 men's, I'd say). Worry and relief followed their leave and return, as if I'd temporarily misplaced my keys. Unexpected turns caused me to second-guess my partner's strategy. Why turn left there when the trail is so obviously right?

A glance at the altimeter: 7,900 feet. Soil was becoming scarce and so were my friend's impressions. Another hundred feet and the trail turned completely to rock, smooth andesite formed in inch-thick plates and broken like crockery. Shards of the stuff jutted out over the Emmons a few yards to my left. It was loose and slippery. It was getting steeper. It was growing late. Clouds skirred up the Emmons and began to veil Mount Ruth. I strapped my ski poles to my pack and scrambled on all fours. I realized I had left my ice axe in the car: stupidity defined. A shard slipped beneath my boot and flooded my mind with an imagined sense-memory: I was tumbling backwards down the talus, in control only of my voice, which I heard expel the words "Oh God oh God please" in a remarkably calm tone.

In a few minutes the clouds had grown so thick around me that the only way to estimate the magnitude of my disorientation was to take an altimeter reading and cross-check it with a topo map. Altimeter: 8,220 feet. Check the map. Camp Curtis is at 8,200 feet. So where the hell was I? Going up to meet, at 8,250 feet, my limit.

The andesite ended abruptly at an outcropping of basalt cinder, molten rock thrown up by the volcano and cooled into a dark rust color with the texture of cauliflower. My phantom partner, it turned out, was a rock climber. I was not. At five o'clock I had two choices. Take my life in my fingertips on the basalt or hazard the steep snowfield without an ice axe. Having read forty years of *Accidents in North American Mountaineering*, I couldn't help assessing my situation in that publication's judgmental terms. Were I to slip, my life would be reduced to a headline: "INEXPERIENCED, ILL EQUIPPED, LOST, ALONE."

I chose a third way: descent. That place of snow and basalt and wind that carried no scent save a slight whiff of fear—that was where I quit with dignity and health. I snapped a quick photo of myself and my terrain to provide clues for the anthropologists who would recover my body centuries hence from the glacier. I zipped up an extra layer of fleece and plunge-stepped down the snowfield.

Twenty minutes later, among the dwarf vegetables, I passed Pam Cox on her way up. She read me like a tabloid.

"Follow somebody else's footprints?"

Yes. Yes, I did.

"Uh-uh. The trail cuts across the snowfield below where you were. It's a pretty easy traverse. You just gotta stay under the ridgeline." She invited me to fall in with her to Camp Curtis, where she was staying the night. This was a kind offer, one that might have been impolite to refuse. But at the moment, well—if the only way to decline her offer had been to bore through the earth to China, I would have dug with my teeth. Once made, the decision to return to the pleasures of home—the warm bed, the soft company—could not be reversed. I did what I had to do. I lied.

"You know, I'm just not feeling that good. Maybe the altitude. Think I'll call it a day. Tell Gator not to send a search party for me."

Quitter.

Cox climbed on, and when she disappeared behind the ridge I let The Renegade fall to the ground. My body followed. I made a bed of pumice, with pieces sized from baby teeth to cannonballs. The Lord is my shepherd I shall not want. He leadeth me to lie down in green pastures. I love to lie down in green pastures. I love to live.

That night at home I lay awake reconsidering my whole idea of the mountain. Far from engendering pride in my daring run up the ridge, the Mount Ruth episode forced me to face the essential folly of my pursuit. Had I taken a fatal tumble onto the Emmons, my death would have set off a chain reaction of human suffering. My new girlfriend and soon-to-be fiancée, who indulged me in my Rainier forays beyond all reasonable limit, would call my parents and friends, who would wait by the phone and squeeze each other's hands and feel apprehension swell into alarm, then fear, and finally dread. Gator and his team would be sent to find me, in the dark, on late summer ice, and it would be no comfort to him that he was on duty this time. At my funeral people would say I died doing what I loved, and they would be lying. I would have died because, as Scott Fischer could have told them if he were alive, I made the wrong choice. I would have died for stupid reasons.

This is the missing piece in the puzzle of mountain climbing, I think. When climbers die, their deaths may make sense to those who share their passion for the highest peaks. But the web of human concern that each of us spins extends much further than we suppose. Those of us who choose not to risk our lives in the mountains are left with the taste of ashes. We are left without friends, wives, husbands, fathers, mothers. We are left with memories never realized.

Maybe I'd been looking in the wrong place. Perhaps the source of Rainier's power over the imagination of the Pacific Northwest, over *my* imagination, was not to be found on the mountain itself. For all my time there, I couldn't help feeling that the closer I got, the further Rainier retreated. This is a visual fact, of course: the higher you climb, the less mountain there is to gaze up at. But the great love we low-landers feel for Rainier, we who know it as the giant on the horizon, exists without the experience of scrambling about its shoulders. Just as the psychic bond with a home develops because our life passes within its four walls, so we become attached to Rainier because it is the single recognizable feature of the landscape within which our lives flourish and expire. Its great height bestows prominence and its imperfect shape adds character. Were it to sink within reach of its Cascade siblings, Rainier would disappear from the regional psyche.

The mountain is *there*, it's a singular object in a way that the forests and the rain and the sea are not. And it's there, if not forever, then at least for as long as we can remember and as long as the longest family memory has been alive. The mountain receives our experiences and becomes part of us; we imprint our memories upon it and trust it with the dearest divisions of our lives. Mount Rainier does not exist under our feet. Mount Rainier lives in our minds.

GOING UP

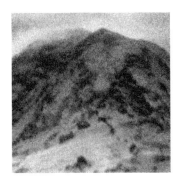

O nly one thing left to do. *Climb the mountain.* There was no question of greater interest than *Will you, Have you, When did you, Why don't you?* Pallid book clerks asked with mild disbelief, as if the challenge were unthinkable for a fellow Ichabod like myself. Crusty mountaineers put it to me like border guards demanding papers. The RMI guides who swapped climbing stories over six-egg omelettes in Ashford inquired with the nonchalance of men who wanted me to pick them up a pack of smokes at the store. *Goin' up?*

I toyed with the idea of deliberately *not* climbing, of standing against the broad-chested culture in which the proving of one's *cojones* was a full-time job and whose heroes tended to be, in a word, dead. I respected the Native American spiritual injunction against climbing the mountain, but couldn't claim it as my own. Neither reason was enough to hold me back. What made me hesitate was fear—the fear of losing something valuable just as it was starting to bloom. The closer my scheduled climb came, the better a budding relationship with a wonderful woman seemed to go and the more I dreaded leaving.

Still, there remained the summit, the only part of the mountain I didn't know. And there was my father. More than anything, in the end I decided to climb for him.

My father was born in the mill town of Everett, Washington, graduated from Everett High School, went to Washington State University, and courted a girl from Everett. After graduation they returned to Everett and got married. His father ran a paint store and once took Senator Henry Jackson fishing on the boat named for his wife, the *Dorothy B.* After selling soft goods and housewares for twenty years at J. C. Penney, my father quit and went into business with my sister's fiancé. If you arrive early for a Seattle Mariners game, you can stop by their stand outside the Kingdome and he'll sell you a bag of peanuts and some Cracker Jacks and tell you how Alex Rodriguez has been hitting that week. He's usually got a couple of tickets in his pocket, and some days we go to the game.

Like many fathers and sons, we bridged our incompatible worlds with the language of sports. Years ago when we lived in Alaska (Dad worked at the Anchorage Penney's store), my grandfather flew up from Everett to fish the king salmon run at the Kenai Peninsula. I remember standing on the beach looking out at the boats in Kachemak Bay and wondering which held my father and grandfather. They returned with a fifty-five-pound king, which they displayed in a photograph that hangs in my parents' home. The old man grimaces from the weight. My grandfather died the next year. Every time I see that picture I smell the warm familiarity of his clothes and wonder if he would have been as happy to catch nothing and just fish with his son.

We reserved a three-day climb with Rainier Mountaineering for early July 1996, and Dad began shedding years of sloth from his legs. Four months before the ascent, I took him up the switchbacks of Rampart Ridge. Dad gasped up the trail and the next day began hiking around his neighborhood wearing a backpack loaded with rocks. Two months later we took a shakedown cruise to Camp Muir. Pushing up the final section of the snowfield, we stopped a dozen times to let him catch his breath and calm his heart, which felt as if it would pump right through his chest. *Goddamn it,* I thought, *this is stupid.* He should have turned around but he couldn't. That close to camp, with his son alongside, he'd push ahead until his heart seized. There were moments when I believed it would.

I called my mother. "Look," I said, "I'm not going up with him unless a doctor checks him out. Lungs, heart, everything. I don't want to kill my own father." He had an appointment later that month, she assured me. She'd make sure he showed up.

A week before the trip, Dad called and said he'd spun the doctor's head. "Said I had the heart of a fifteen-year-old, healthier than ninety-nine percent of guys my age." Mom confirmed the report and told me that Dad was taking the backpack everywhere now, even wearing it on a treadmill at the health club. For the first time I felt that we had a real chance of making it up. My father's desire to climb the mountain was so strong that it had crushed one of the deepest instincts bred in the human bone: the sense to not look silly in front of the neighbors.

Learning to climb a mountain is like repeating infancy. First you master the act of breathing, move on to walking, then accept the challenge of falling down without bonking your head. Before the long walk to Camp Muir, my father and I and most of our expedition mates spent a day studying the basics of glacier travel with George Dunn, one of RMI's most experienced guides. A tall, laid-back fellow with teeth a size too big for his mouth, Dunn had climbed to the top of Mount Rainier more than anyone in the world: three hundred sixty-two times. A record like that is usually accompanied by the phrase "nobody else even comes close," but that summer Dunn and fellow RMI guide Phil Ershler were dueling for the title.

Dunn taught us how to stay alive up high. To compensate for the lack of oxygen at high altitude, it's imperative to pressure-breathe, which involves forcing air out of the lungs with a powerful pump of the gut. When properly executed, a team of pressure-breathing climbers sounds like a roll call of the hearing-impaired: "WHO! WHO! WHO!" The rest step, the trademark of a Lou Whittaker–trained guide, uses the least possible amount of energy and muscle strain to achieve a single elevated step. Instead of pushing off the ball of the left foot while lifting with the quadricep muscles at the front of the thigh, as in a normal step, the body's weight is shifted to the forward leg while the back leg lifts up to the next step using the momentum of the weight shift. The trailing foot barely clears the ground, and the lower half of the leg kicks in as if hung on an oiled hinge. A rest-stepper looks as if he's got ten-pound weights tied to his boots.

Finally, Dunn schooled us in the finer points of falling. The most important act of a plummeting mountaineer, besides digging the pick of his ice axe into the snow, is to yell, *"Falling!"* to alert his rope team that they have approximately two seconds to plunge their own axes into the mountain before two hundred pounds of tumble jerks their bodies into space. This is more difficult than it sounds. Our entire lives are spent learning to deflect attention from our own mistakes. Alerting the rope team requires breaking that conditioning and announcing your own mishap, one that may botch the entire year-in-the-planning expedition, *while it is happening.* Mountain travel favors the shameless over the shy. My father, who had spent decades winning the confidence of strangers on the sales floor, was particularly adept at the skill. *Falling!*

A Park Service guide to Mount Rainier published in 1930 contained a caution to tourists whose ambition outstripped their experience. "Mount Rainier is not an easy climb. The great altitude of its summit...and the low level of the region about its base (between 2,000 and 5,000 feet) combine to make the ascent an exceedingly long and exhausting one. Dangerously crevassed ice covers a large portion of the mountain's flanks, while the sharp ridges between the glaciers are composed of treacherous crumbling lava and pumice. Those who have set their ambition on making the ascent will do well, therefore, to realize at the outset that there is no choice of routes, and that should one lose the beaten trail there is little or no hope of extricating oneself by another way."

About ten thousand people attempt to climb Mount Rainier every year; fewer than fifty-five hundred succeed. Some people have tried five or six times and failed to summit. Some days it's the altitude, some days it's the weather, some days it's the will.

On the morning of our summit climb, the RMI guidehouse was as chaotic as the first day of school. Climbers packed and repacked their equipment, turning the floor into a colorful quilt of jackets, mittens, gaiters, and hats. Alex Van Steen, our lead guide, interrogated each of his nineteen clients: Have you got everything on the equipment list? The big down jacket? Overmittens? Water bottle? It was a game of bullshitting; each of us had at least one piece of equipment that, as a carpenter friend of mine would say, wasn't up to code. My father had rented an enormous North Face down parka, the retail price of which could procure waterfront property. I had skimped on the parka, instead packing a thin green jacket that would throw a chill into a penguin and was two sizes too small besides. I held a corner of this Lime Fakey up to Van Steen and he checked me through without a second look.

Every once in a while the climbing rangers at Camp Muir and Camp Schurman meet ill-equipped climbers who insist that wool pants and hiking boots were good enough for the pioneers and they'll be good enough for them. "That's when you have to explain that what you don't read about those early ascents was their incredibly high failure rate," Gator once told me. On the first recorded ascent of Rainier's glaciers in 1857, August Kautz and two companions carried alpenstocks hewn of dry ash, one fifty-foot rope, one thermometer, and a tin canteen each. They wore their heaviest woolens and sewed an extra sole upon their shoes, spiked with four-penny nails. Meals consisted of dried beef and hardtack, a flour-and-water biscuit that became the staple of the Old West for its imperishability and a perennial source of complaint for its unpalatability.

Our own gear would have astonished August Kautz: sweat-wicking synthetic longjohns, jackets and pants made of a material called "fleece" (with no apology to the sheep), down-filled parkas, Gore-Tex jackets and rain pants, two pairs of socks, three pairs of mittens, two hats, plastic climbing boots, nylon gaiters, steel crampons, plastic helmet, battery-powered headlamp, and scarred metal ice axe. Our food was freeze-dried or ground into mealy chocolate-flavored Power-Bars. Nineteenth-century climbers often carried three-foot-tall barometers to measure the altitude; our altimeters fit on our wrists.

While we scrambled to perfect our kits, the guides introduced themselves. Alex Van Steen, a veteran of more than eighty trips up Rainier (every guide keeps an exact tally), was a stern sergeant. His oven-browned face bore the imprint of years of mountain travel. Glacier glasses preserved a raccoon mask of delicate pink around his eyes. As the lead guide Van Steen held ultimate responsibility for nineteen lives for two days on one of the most dangerous mountains in America. It was not a duty he took lightly, and he apologized for his authoritarian bearing. "Sometimes I think I'm a pretty scary guy," he told us. In the off season Van Steen taught people how to climb frozen waterfalls.

Our senior guide, Eric Simonson, stood quietly against a far wall rubbing sunscreen into his face and arms. Simonson was approaching the three-hundred-summit mark. In the off season he operated a guide service that took clients to Aconcagua, Mount McKinley, the Himalayas, Antarctica, and the Swiss Alps. He and his wife also owned the Overland Restaurant and Inn in Ashford. I often ran into him over a plate of eggs. When you first meet him, Simonson strikes you as the kind of unassuming guy who designs hinges for Boeing. On the mountain he is a charging bear. He can pull a client straight up a glacier and isn't bashful about doing it. My rope leader was Jason Tanguay, a twenty-year-old apprentice guide and biology student at Whitman College in Walla Walla.

The nineteen clients were a mix of paramedics, firemen, dentists, doctors, writers, and students. There was Sam, a digital-imaging professor from the Rochester Institute of Technology whose name was embroidered on his pack; David, an Orting city councilman who wanted to stand on top of the mountain that was poised to destroy his town; Diane, a United Airlines flight attendant whose high-altitude workplace I envied more and more the higher we climbed; Viraj, a San Diego schoolteacher whose boots cut into her feet like can openers; Dan, a Miami psychologist who wore high-fashion sunglasses and a dashing salt-and-pepper beard; and Dan the Camo Man, a Kentucky nurse-anesthetist who carried his water in 1500cc saline bottles and dressed in army Arctic fatigues. Some had climbed Aconcagua and Mount Whitney, some had climbed stairs.

Under a dazzling midmorning sun we tramped out from Paradise, the clop of our climbing boots warning the day trippers in our path to step aside. Our route would take us up to Camp Muir the first day, then continue early the next morning across the Cowlitz Glacier, through a notch in Cathedral Rocks Ridge, up the sloping ridge of loose rock to the Ingraham Glacier, across the hazardous Ingraham Icefall, up the switchbacks of Disappointment Cleaver, and finally up the last two thousand vertical feet of ice to the summit. Old guides called it the dog run.

Friends who'd warned me against RMI said the guides would put us through a forced march straight up the mountain. They were correct. We took ten-minute breaks every hour and a half, no exceptions, which was the only way to move two dozen people up a 14,000-foot peak in less than twenty-eight hours.

"Watch me," Alex told us. "When I sit, you sit. We're going to be walking up this mountain all day. Give your legs a break when you can."

Standing at rest break became the equivalent of chewing gum in class. "Viraj, why are you standing?" Alex scolded. Viraj sat.

We made slow progress, each of us carrying the equivalent of a six-year-old child on our backs. My father and I didn't speak much but checked on each other. I made sure he drank more water than he thought he needed; he gave me one of his tuna sandwiches.

Our wilting platoon shuffled into Camp Muir at a quarter to five that afternoon. The guides huddled in the RMI cookshack while the rest of us jockeyed for bed space in the plywood bunkhouse. Our quarters consisted of an unheated room shelved with racks three deep in a sort of Third World barracks style.

A few minutes after we shed our packs, the air in our little mountain castle filled with the steam of instant soup and freeze-dried stroganoff. Dad and I shared a double helping of packet-ready beef teriyaki. As we chased the last grains of rice, the junior guides instructed us in the art of harness buckling, before yielding the floor to Alex, who gave us a climbing-eve pep talk. "We'll be monitoring the weather all night, and I'll let you know how to dress in the morning. Right now it looks pretty good, not much wind. But things change fast." He explained the use of a Park Service "blue bag" for the call of nature (crap and carry), but said we wouldn't have time to stop for a squat on the way up. "I suggest you squeeze one out before we leave."

"Finally. And this is extremely important. At every stop we're going to ask you how you're doing. We are not just making conversation. You need to answer quickly and honestly."

He called out the rope team rosters, four or five climbers on each. Friends and relatives, he said, would tie in to separate teams to make sure they stayed friendly and related by the end of the trip. My father and I would not climb together.

I snugged my watchcap over my head a few minutes before seven that night and climbed into my third-shelf bunk to find a few hours' sleep. At my feet Dan the Camo Man lashed his body to the wall. He had claimed the most precarious perch in the shed, a high catwalk between sleeping platforms, in order to snatch a few threads of breeze drifting through a window. Dan looked at me and smiled; the accommodations suited him.

Sleep that night was as rare as the air. I stared at the timbers of our ramshackle hotel and listened to the concert of sighs, wheezes, snorts, and sniffles that played through the night. Every once in a while I heard my father clear his throat on the bunk below. I took comfort in the familiar sound, as I always have. Many evenings of my childhood were spent roaming through J. C. Penney, squatting under a bank of television sets, fondling the bicycles, or fingerwalking through the record bins. Wherever I was, my father's phlegmatic call alerted me to his presence. No worries.

August Kautz never made it to the summit back in 1857. He came within a few hundred feet before high winds and the lateness of the day defeated his attempt. By the time they returned to Fort Steila-coom, the men in Kautz's party were so haggard and sunburnt that none of their acquaintances recognized them. Their clothes hung in tatters. The hat blown off Kautz's head near the summit had been replaced by the sleeve of his red flannel shirt, "tied into a knot at the elbow, with the point at the arm-pit for a visor." One of his companions wore a coffee sack for pants.

Thirteen years passed before Philemon Beecher Van Trump and Hazard Stevens reached the true summit in 1870. Van Trump was an Ohio-born prospector who came West as the private secretary of the territorial governor, Marshall Moore. Stevens was the son of the first territorial governor, Isaac Stevens, whose term was consumed by Indian wars. At the age of thirteen, Hazard Stevens had accompanied his father on the treaty-making expeditions of 1854 and 1855, and later fought alongside him at the Battle of Chantilly in 1862. Hazard caught Confederate fire in his arm and hip. His father was cut down by a bullet to the temple in the midst of a reckless charge. "He fell dead," recorded Stevens's biographer Kent Richards, "clutching the [Union] colors in his hands."

Stevens, Van Trump, and Edmund Coleman, the party's third member who dropped out early in the ascent due to equipment trouble (he lost his backpack), happened upon their Yakama guide Sluiskin along the Cowlitz River, where he had camped with his wife and two children. Sluiskin's wardrobe blended elements of Eastern fancy with the hides of passing deer. A plain buckskin shirt comple-mented the striped wool breechclout that dressed his loins. On his head he wore a military cap whose visor was thickly studded with brass-headed nails, and whose crown spouted a fountain of eagle feathers and fur dangles. "Notwithstanding its components," Stevens later wrote, Sluiskin's ensemble "appeared imposing rather than ridiculous." Sluiskin agreed to lead the men along the mountain's lower flanks, where he often hunted deer and mountain goat, but dismissed their plan to scale the summit as absurd.

Stevens and Van Trump could not be dissuaded, however, and when the trio reached the Paradise meadows, Sluiskin decided to end their foolish errand. Following a supper of roasted grouse and coffee, the guide exhorted them in Chinook and broken English to turn back before the mountain swept them away.

Listen to me, my good friends. I must talk to you.

Your plan to climb Takhoma is all foolishness. No one can do it and live. A mighty chief dwells upon the summit in a lake of fire. He brooks no intruders.

Many years ago my grandfather, the greatest and bravest chief of all the Yakama, climbed nearly to the summit. There he caught sight of the fiery lake and the infernal demon coming to destroy him, and he fled down the mountain, glad to escape with his life. Where he failed, no other Indian ever dared make the attempt.

At first the way is easy, the task seems light. The broad snowfields, over which I have often hunted the mountain goat, offer an inviting path. But above them you will have to climb over steep rocks overhanging deep gorges where a misstep would hurl you far down—down to certain death. You must creep over steep snow banks and cross deep crevasses where a mountain goat could hardly keep his footing. You must climb along steep cliffs where rocks are continually falling to crush you, or knock you off into the bottomless depths.

And if you should escape these perils and reach the great snowy dome, then a bitterly cold and furious tempest will sweep you off into space like a withered

leaf. But if by some miracle you should survive all these perils the mighty
demon of Takhoma will surely kill you and throw you into the fiery lake.

Don't go!

Don't go!

Stevens and Van Trump rolled up in their blankets and retired to
sleep beside the simmering fire. They were awakened now and then
by Sluiskin's somber dirge and the thunder of avalanches falling high
above.

Alex woke us at half past midnight. "Good morning," he said. "It's
thirty-eight degrees out and clear, great climbing weather. Go ahead
and get dressed, eat some breakfast. Here's what I want you to wear.
On your legs I want fleece pants and nothing else. No underwear.
Wear a light shirt up top, no jacket. Fleece gloves on your hands. I
want you sticking to that snow if you fall."

His instructions baffled me. Climb without underwear? It took a
ten-count to thaw my brain: *long* underwear. I kept my shorts on.

Dad sipped a cup of hot bouillon and ate a few bites of the granola-
and-powdered-milk cereal I'd packed, which, he later told me, tasted
terrible. "How you doing?" I asked.

"Good. I didn't sleep at all, but I'm feeling all right. You?"

"Feeling great."

"Let's go get it."

Harness, boots, crampons, helmet, headlamp. Where the hell were
those fleece gloves? I rummaged through The Renegade once, twice,
finding nothing, holding back the rising panic of a man whose father's

midlife ambition was about to be scuttled by a pair of seventeen-dollar mitts. The senior guides barked hurry-ups to the younger crew.

Chris Booher, the young guide who was leading my father's rope team, happened by on his way from the outhouse. "Chris, Chris," I said apologetically. "I can't find my fleece gloves. I've gone all through my pack and I just—" and at this point my hands, fumbling blindly through a lower pocket, struck a familiar softness—"ah, I just *found* my gloves." Chris smiled and continued on, no doubt relieved that he wouldn't be tending my idiocy all the way to the summit.

There are few more thrilling moments in life than the first steps of a summit day (which actually begins in the middle of the night). Even the satisfaction of topping out cannot match it. Under a brilliant moon you step onto a shadowy glacier, matching your rope partners step for step, your heart pumping equal parts apprehension and adrenaline to the ends of your fingers and toes, and all you can hear is the sound of your boots shattering thousands of crystals and your mouth blowing the moist airwaste of your lungs up to heaven. *Crunch crunch huff. Crunch crunch huff.* Ahead, the headlamps of twenty-four mountaineers string across the Cowlitz Glacier to Cathedral Gap like lights on a Christmas tree. And you think, *My God what am I doing here.*

The advantage of climbing Mount Rainier in July is the weather. We climbed to the summit wearing T-shirts. The disadvantage is scree, the loose sand and rock on the ridges that separate the mountain's glaciers, which in winter and spring is covered by snow. As we ascended the rocky fence separating the Cowlitz and the Ingraham Glaciers, our steel crampons slipped in the sand and glanced off the rocks, sparking fireflies into the night. Ropes wrapped around rocks and tangled in legs. Jason Tanguay, our rope guide, shouted encouragement above us. My ropemates—the talkative schoolteacher Viraj and two quiet men I came to know as John I and John II—and I scrambled and cursed on hands and knees to catch up.

"Shit!"

"Sorry."

"Son of a *bitch*."

We reached our first conclusion of the day: rock bad, snow good.

We climbed an hour and a half before resting in the early morning darkness on the Ingraham Flats, a relatively safe section of the Ingraham Glacier, one mile away from Camp Muir.

"Packs off! Parkas on!" yelled Alex. I dropped The Renegade, which was uncharacteristically light without its usual garage of sleeping bags, tents, stoves, and food. I couldn't wrap the Lime Fakey around me fast enough. At two-thirty in the morning on a high mountain glacier, it was cold enough to curse.

The guides surveyed their teams. Viraj, the two Johns, and I were still running full steam. Other teams were losing links. Tiffany, a woman on my father's rope, admitted she didn't have anything left, and the senior guides leapt into action. "Let's go! Get that bag out, move her off the rope!" yelled Eric Simonson, who cracked the whip all the way up the mountain. Tiffany the Climber became Tiffany the Bag and Tag, the ignominious designation for exhausted mountaineers who are stuffed into a sleeping bag, dug into a safe snowbed, and left to their own loneliness as the rest of the team moves on.

Our own destiny lay beneath the Ingraham Icefall, the most dangerous section on the mountain's safest route. An icefall is a steep section of glacier, a sort of solid waterfall in which the forward motion of the ice combines with the day's melt to send many-ton blocks crashing down the field. It was near here in 1981 that ten climbers and an RMI guide were killed in an avalanche that began when a serac high on the edge of the glacier toppled onto the steep slope and triggered a catastrophic slide of ice and snow. All eleven victims remain buried within the glacier.

"We've got to move through this section quickly," Jason told John I, who relayed the message to Viraj, who told it to me, who passed it to John II. Jason could have skipped the order. The trail across the icefall was ten inches wide, enough for one boot but not quite two, so it was impossible to remain balanced without continuous motion. Looking up from the trail was enough to unbalance one's nerve. Ice blocks from previous falls studded the steep white pitch to our left; to the right the icefield dropped as if the mountain was running away from itself.

Now we moved up the switchbacks of Disappointment Cleaver and through our last reserves of energy. The adrenaline we felt on Cathedral Rocks was displaced by fatigue and nausea. Our progress was too slow for the guides, who vented their frustration on a party of independent climbers in their path. "What's the holdup up there?" Alex asked. "Coupla irritants with gear trouble," replied Eric, using RMI slang for nonguided parties. It's a free mountain, but nobody clocks as much time between Muir and the summit as the RMI guides, and they tend to be a little proprietary about the route. Run ahead of them or walk behind them, but do not stand in their way.

Disappointment Cleaver is an island of rock overlooking the vast ice chasm of the Emmons Glacier. As far as local historians can tell, its name comes from the reaction of climbers who navigate its steep flanks only to find themselves thousands of feet below the summit. Sucking wind and stemming a rising tide of nausea, I stumbled the last few steps into what would be our expedition's point of reckoning. "That mountain proved a severer task than we anticipated," observed August Kautz after his 1857 attempt. Nowhere did his words ring truer than on the Cleaver, 12,500 feet high. The night sky yielded to day and turned an eerie shade of salmon bisque. We gazed down on Mount Adams to the south; to the east, Yakima and Spokane awoke to brilliant views of the mountain, with our battered crew crouched upon it.

We switched off our lamps and sat, never so spent in our lives. Our limbs shivered from fatigue and the cold, but were less of a concern than our minds, which were battered and benumbed by the climb. Nothing in the world mattered anymore except the simple act of survival. I don't have to die doing this, I told myself. At that moment I imagined my father and me bagging and tagging at the Cleaver, lying together in the snow to watch the sun greet the new world.

First, though, food. I took a bite of a half-frozen peanut butter and jelly sandwich, chewed twice, gagged, and spat. I had the appetite of a seasick lubber. My energy bars were savory as sawdust. My stomach finally accepted a handful of dried apple and pear slices. The sugar buoyed me enough that I considered continuing on.

"Only an idiot swims a mile out to sea without enough energy to swim back in," Alex hollered at our bedraggled company. "You must have enough gas to get up and come back down. Be honest with yourself."

Soldiers were falling. I looked toward my father, who sat in the snow staring at his tuna sandwich as if it had spoken. He set the sandwich in the snow, glanced at me, and looked out over the bumpy land that ran to Idaho and Oregon and beyond. On his face was an expression of confusion and betrayal, as if the fatigue and mountain sickness he had trained so hard to ward off had found him anyway. He felt himself moving in slow motion. By the time he dug his parka out of his pack at the beginning of the rest break, the guides were already tucking theirs back in and loading up to move. Alex, Eric, and Chris knelt and told him they were worried about him making it down safely. It was his decision, they said. Dad nodded and the three guides moved on to his ropemate Sam, the Rochester professor, who was experiencing dizzy spells.

I unclipped my carabiner and walked over, taking care not to stumble into a peeing climber. "How you doing?"

He sighed and spoke slowly. "I can't eat."

"Have you tried—"

"No. I can't get anything in my stomach. I can't even drink water."

Neither of us could say the words "turn around," but we knew his climb was over. Without food or water his body would collapse. I wrapped my arms around him and hugged him tight. "Proud of you," I said. We had time for a quick snapshot before the guides split the party. Half went down with my father, half went up with me. The only thing keeping me from turning back was the thought that I might have to return to this dismal ground. Near the summit of Mount Fuji there is a signboard that bears an old Japanese saying: "Only a fool has never climbed Mount Fuji; only a fool has climbed it more than once." I needed that once.

John I became disoriented and, for the sake of the rest of us, dropped out twenty paces above the Cleaver. Our team stood at four. Jason led Viraj, me, and John II through a garden of seracs—huge ice towers—that bloomed around us on the bright white plain. Breathing became an obsession. "Your lungs are directly attached to your legs.

Breathe!" Eric shouted to one lagging climber. We walked up steep sections with our feet splayed like ducks for better balance. We hopped over crevasses to which there was no bottom, only an ever-deepening tone of blue. Viraj and I bonded over a Payday bar, which I offered her frozen from my pocket. Up the final thousand feet, each step required a full breath of air.

When you stand in it, the summit crater looks like a bowl of Cream of Wheat big enough for forty football teams to play twenty football games and still have room for concessions. Piles of infant rocks rim the crater, kept free of snow by the constant wind and the volcano's steam heat. When Van Trump and Stevens arrived here more than one hundred twenty-five years ago, Stevens found himself in a scene reminiscent of Wagnerian opera. "On every side of the mountain were deep gorges falling off precipitously thousands of feet, and from these the thunderous sound of avalanches would rise occasionally," he wrote. "The wind was now a perfect tempest, and bitterly cold; smoke and mist were flying about the base of the mountain, half hiding, half revealing its gigantic outlines; and the whole scene was sublimely awful."

I felt nothing sublime or awful. By the time we reached the top, reaching the top no longer mattered, if it ever had at all. The twelve of us shrugged off our packs and bundled up against the twenty-degree chill. I pulled on a fleece top and the Lime Fakey and a Gore-Tex shell and bundled each hand in three mittens and still shivered the morning in. Jason led those who could muster the energy on a half-hour trek to sign the summit register. The rest of us exchanged feeble high-fives and sat in the morning breeze, content to rest our legs in the snow. We smiled for the camera but not for ourselves. I found myself caring about nothing except the rudiments of survival: warmth, water, and food. My mind had entered a latitude of apathy and despair. Hiking to the register seemed a ridiculous waste of energy. I was here; would my signature prove anything more? Retrieving a camera from my backpack required a monumental force of will, and the few snapshots that returned from 14,000 feet were taken only for my mother, because I didn't care about recording the scene. On top of the mountain I knew very few things. I knew I wanted to get down. I knew that sometimes rites of passage, like the experience of suffering, lead to great wisdom. And sometimes suffering in the wilderness is just suffering in the wilderness and the only wisdom you gain is the knowledge that you don't want to do it again. Finally, I knew I wanted to see the people I loved. Badly. Terribly. I wanted to see my father.

For nearly an hour we sat there detached and withdrawn, offering few words to our companions. Dan the Camo Man, who had run through his rations on the way up, traded his forty-four-dollar head-lamp for a handful of Eric's cookies.

Most people who die on mountains are killed on the way down. The muscles are weary and the mind goes lax. If an ascending climber stumbles, he can catch himself on the uphill slope. When a descending climber hooks a crampon on a gaiter, he will fly into the air with the forces of gravity and forward motion allied against him. For the acrophobic there is the added element of light. In darkness the danger is concealed; at midmorning all is revealed. Clenching a fixed rope over one of the route's trickier sections, I weighed three decades of personal folly and found none that surpassed my present predicament. "This," I said aloud, "is the stupidest thing I've ever done."

On through the serac yard and over the Cleaver, legs trembling like sinners before God. At the Ingraham Icefall, a traffic jam. Seeing a chance to soothe my crying quadriceps, I squatted while the climbers ahead prepared to thread the fall. Jason nipped my mutiny before it spread up the rope. "DO NOT SIT DOWN!"

Okay.

In the six hours since we'd last crossed the icefall the world had warmed considerably. Precarious seracs frozen tight to the glacier began to melt free and roll, initiating a game of mountain roulette. Alex's team went first, followed by Jason's, then Eric's. Our sluggish ascent and the balmy morning had put an edge on our guides' attitudes. They did not like crossing this late in the day.

"Gotta move your guys faster, Jason!" Eric dug in the spurs.

John II stumbled through a nasty rock scree. Behind me Viraj struggled to keep pace. I couldn't look back but I didn't have to. A climbing rope is a telegraph wire between two climbers. A trailing climber's slightest falter registers as a tug at her teammate's waist. By the time we pulled back in to Camp Muir, I could sense the difference between a sneeze and a cough.

"Tell your crew to pick it up, Jason!"

I yelled a word or two of encouragement to John II and tried to convey my sympathy. The devil had sliced several inches from the trail before our return; our ice axes found little purchase. So many climbers had used the trail that the snowbank had turned into a Swiss cheese of axe holes. Sometimes your axe struck firm, sometimes it slid in to the hilt. John II and I moved under the ice in a walking trot and I prayed *God, don't let me stumble now.*

"GO! GO! GO! GO! GO!" Eric was unrelenting.

"You gotta move faster, John!" said Jason.

I imagined my hand snapping the comments out of the air before they could reach John's ears. The man was at the tottery edge of control. One more crack of the whip was likely to send him tripping down the icefall, taking me along as his first victim.

Besides, I couldn't go any faster myself.

"Come on now, thirty more yards," I said under my breath as the Ingraham Flats came into view. "Twenty. Ten. Good man, John."

Ten minutes after clearing the icefall we sat on the Ingraham Flats and watched two ice chunks the size of UPS vans calve and roll a thousand feet down the glacier, directly through our vacated path. Alex said it was the biggest icefall he'd ever seen on Rainier.

Sluiskin was so certain Van Trump and Stevens would die on the mountain that, before they went, he demanded they write a note to the authorities in Olympia absolving him of responsibility. Their subsequent return did not prompt spontaneous celebration. "Seeing us for the first time, [Sluiskin] stopped short, gazed long and fixedly, and then slowly drew near, eyeing us closely the while, as if to see whether we were real flesh and blood or disembodied ghosts fresh from the evil demon of Takhoma," reported Stevens. Both Rainier pioneers published accounts of their harrowing ascent, but locals still grumbled, "I'd like to see them prove it." After incredulous locals scoffed at his account of a solo ascent of Rainier's Willis Wall in 1961, an Eastern mountaineer named Charlie Bell came back the next year and climbed it again, this time with a camera.

Our own return to Paradise passed with no skepticism and a disheartening lack of fanfare. Climbing Mount Rainier has become so routine that the world takes notice only when climbers with seemingly insurmountable handicaps make the ascent. Rock climbers in Seattle had scoffed at Rainier, told me it was nothing but a long walk. They were wrong. It was brutal. As we walked across the Cowlitz Glacier within sight of Camp Muir, I heard a climber ask Eric about other mountains to climb. "You might want to think about McKinley," Eric said. *You might want to check your sanity*, I thought. John Muir had it right: Mountains aren't best known from their frozen tops, so far from home so high in the sky.

I saw my father. Standing near the Muir guide hut apart from the crowd sunning themselves on the rocks, he squinted into the sun and tried to pick me out of the necklace moving across the glacier. I have never been so happy to see him. After taking the last few steps, I unlocked my carabiner and hugged him as I've never hugged him before, and said over and over, *It's so good to see you. It's so good to see you. It's so good to see you.*

ACKNOWLEDGMENTS

In the course of writing this book I've incurred debts to many generous and helpful people. My thanks go to those scientists, historians, rangers, and researchers who aided my research, many of whom are mentioned here and some of whom are not. At Mount Rainier National Park, special thanks to Mike Gauthier and the climbing rangers, and to Kathleen Jobson, Regina Rochefort, Julie Hover, Ann Bell, Gary Ahlstrand, Darin Swinney, Bill Dengler, John Krambrink, Roger Drake, Dixie Gatchel, Rich Lechleitner, Barbara Samora, and Ben Olver. Scientists at the USGS Cascades Volcano Observatory who patiently tutored me included Kevin Scott, Steve Brantley, and Carolyn Dreidger. Tom Sisson, Rocky Crandell, Bill Lokey, Steve Malone, Seth Moran, and Robert Tilling also brought me up to speed on the volcano. Credit should be laid at their feet, blame at mine.

Jane Bromet was an invaluable climbing source, as were Karen Dickinson, Peter Goldman, Todd Burleson, and Ed Viesturs. I wish Scott Fischer was still around to thank. Jim Litch, Stefan Goldberg, Robert "Brownie" Schoene, Tom Hornbein, and Brenda Townes generously answered my queries about high altitude. Ralph Squillace and Cecelia Svinth Carpenter offered their historical expertise, and Reid Coen showed me where the records were buried in the archives. A high marmot call goes out to David Barash and Dan Blumstein. Thanks to Laura Walls, to whom I owe an entirely separate book, and also to John Edwards, Ed Lisowski, Ake and Bronka Sundstrom, Carolyn Pope, Bruce Meyers, Ron Coffey, Gene Harvey, Margaret Wurtele, Luke Reinsma, Father Timothy Sauer, Tim Gregg, Paul Tough, Brenda Peterson, Jonathon Storm, Dee Molenaar, Lou Whittaker, and Rainier Mountaineering Incorporated.

Special thanks are owed to Gary Luke and Elizabeth Wales, who helped conceive this book and bring it to fruition. Janice Bultmann gave me the early readings and encouragement to keep going, and Katherine Koberg and David Brewster provided the time to write. Skip Card hit the trail when nobody else would and doused me when I caught fire. Thanks finally to Claire Dederer for providing love, patience, understanding, and inspiration.

NOTES ON SOURCES

A handful of Rainier books kept me company during my months at the mountain, including *The Challenge of Rainier*, by the great mountaineer and mapmaker Dee Molenaar; *Mountain Fever: Historic Conquests of Rainier*, by Aubrey L. Haines; *Mount Rainier: A Record of Exploration*, edited by the early Northwest historian Edmond S. Meany; *The Big Fact Book About Mount Rainier*, an up-to-date Rainier encyclopedia by Bette Filley; *Cascade Alpine Guide 1: Columbia River to Stevens Pass*, a detailed climbing route guide by Fred Beckey, and *Mountaineering: The Freedom of the Hills*, a comprehensive climbing source edited by Don Graydon.

Readers considering doing all or part of the Wonderland Trail would do well to purchase a copy of Bette Filley's *Discovering the Wonders of the Wonderland Trail,* a mile-by-mile guide. You might want to cut it up into sections; it worked for me. Ira Spring and Harvey Manning's *50 Hikes in Mount Rainier National Park* serves the same purpose for non-Wonderland jaunts. Catherine Feher-Elston's *Ravensong*, with beautiful illustrations by Lawrence Ormsby, explores both the mythology and science of the mysterious bird. For further reading, see *Ravens in Winter*, by Bernd Heinrich.

I relied heavily upon the work of Nisqually historian Cecelia Svinth Carpenter for information about Native American beliefs about Mount Rainier. Her book, *Where the Waters Begin: The Traditional Nisqually Indian History of Mount Rainier*, is available at Mount Rainier National Park but deserves wider circulation. The Yakama creation story was originally told by Coteeaku, son of Kamiakin, to U.S. Army Major J. W. MacMurray, and recorded by James Mooney in the BAE *Fourteenth Annual Report*, 1892–93. It is reprinted in *Indian Legends of the Pacific Northwest*, by Ella E. 'Clark. For further reading, see *Magic in the*

Mountains: The Yakima Shaman, Power & Practice, by Donald M. Hines; and *Coyote Was Going There: Indian Literature of the Oregon Country*, compiled and edited by Jarold Ramsey.

The Tacoma Public Library's local history files were invaluable in researching the history of the "Mount Tacoma" fight, as was the work of historian Genevieve McCoy. McCoy's "Mount Tacoma vs Mount Rainier: The fight to rename the mountain" appeared in the October 1986 issue of *Pacific Northwest Quarterly*; her more comprehensive master's thesis, "Call It Mount Tacoma," is available at the University of Washington's Suzzallo Library. Two general histories of Tacoma aided my research: *Tacoma, Its History and Its Builders,* by Herbert Hunt; and *Puget's Sound*, by Murray Morgan. The journals of William Fraser Tolmie weren't published until the early 1960s, as *The Journals of William Fraser Tolmie, Physician and Fur Trader*. George Vancouver's 1792 sighting and naming of the mountain is recounted in his three-volume journal, *A Voyage of Discovery to the North Pacific Ocean and Round the World*. The best available portrait of Peter Rainier is published in *Vancouver's Discovery of Puget Sound*, by Edmond S. Meany. The description of Rainier's retirement banquet was found in *The Naval Chronicle*, volume 15 (London, 1806); his single-line obituary comes from the 1808 volume of the same publication. For more reading about Rainier, see *The Royal Navy: A History from the Earliest Times to the Present*, by William Laird Clowes; *The Private Papers of George, Second Earl of Spencer, First Lord of the Admiralty, 1794–1801*, edited by Julian S. Corbett, and the *Dictionary of National Biography*, edited by Sidney Lee.

A number of excellent articles about insects in snow and ice can be found in *Insects at Low Temperature*, Richard E. Lee, Jr., and David L.

Denlinger, editors. Other sources included *The Insects*, Thomas Eisner and Edward O. Wilson, editors; *Insect Behavior*, by Robert W. Matthews and Janice R. Matthews; *Ecology and Biogeography of High Altitude Insects*, by M. S. Mani; *The Ecology of Insect Overwintering*, by S. R. Leather, et al.; and "Arthropods of Alpine Aeolian Ecosystems," by John S. Edwards in the *Annual Review of Entomology*, 1987. The National Audubon Society's *Field Guide to North American Insects and Spiders* was a helpful general reference. Stephen Jay Gould discusses J. B. S. Kenneth Haldane's "inordinate fondness for beetles," and Kermack's clarification, in his book *Dinosaur in a Haystack*. Further discussions of species biodiversity can be found in *Noah's Choice*, by Charles C. Mann and Mark L. Plummer; and "Counting Species One by One," by Nigel Stork and Kevin Gaston, *New Scientist*, August 11, 1990.

Carolyn Dreidger's *A Visitor's Guide to Mount Rainier Glaciers* is a wonderful general guide to the mountain's glaciers. For more in-depth information about glacial behavior see *Glaciers of North America*, by Sue A. Ferguson. Edmond Meany's poem "Carbon Glacier" was published in *The Mountaineer*, 1909. For further reading about Ötzi the ice man, see *The Man in the Ice*, by Konrad Spindler.

The Geologic Story of Mount Rainier, by Dwight R. Crandell, provides a basic overview of the mountain's birth. It's available at Mount Rainier National Park, or in research libraries as *U.S. Geological Survey Bulletin 1292*. For a wider view of Pacific Northwest geology and natural history, see *The Natural History of Puget Sound Country*, by Arthur Kruckeberg; and *Fire Mountains of the West,* by Stephen L. Harris. For information about specific Rainier events, see some of Dwight Crandell's other USGS papers: "Surficial Geology of Mount Rainier National Park, Washington" (*U.S. Geological Survey Bulletin 1288*); "Volcanic

Hazards at Mount Rainier, Washington" (*U.S. Geological Survey Bulletin 1238*, written with D. R. Mullineaux); "Rockfalls and Avalanches from Little Tahoma Peak on Mount Rainier, Washington" (*U.S. Geological Survey Bulletin 1221-A*, written with Robert K. Fahnestock); and "A Recent Volcanic Mudflow of Exceptional Dimensions from Mount Rainier, Washington" (*American Journal of Science*, June 1956, written with H. H. Waldron). Kevin Scott's research (with James Vallance and Pat Pringle) on Rainier flows was published in "Sedimentology, behavior, and hazards of debris flows at Mount Rainier, Washington," *U.S. Geological Survey Professional Paper 1547. Mount Rainier: Active Cascade Volcano*, published by the U.S. Geodynamics Committee of the National Research Council, is a useful report on the potential hazards of Rainier. Detailed information on the summit fumaroles can be found in "Hydrothermal Processes at Mount Rainier, Washington," David Frank's PhD thesis, kept at the University of Washington's Allen Library; a shorter version of Frank's thesis appeared in the *Journal of Volcanology and Geothermal Research*, volume 65 (1995). For general historical information about volcanoes, see *Volcanoes: Fire from the Earth*, by Maurice Krafft. Frank Dawson Adams's *The Birth and Development of the Geological Sciences* provides a wealth of information about the early years of earth science. For information about plate tectonics, see *This Dynamic Earth: The Story of Plate Tectonics*, by W. Jacquelyne Kious and Robert I. Tilling, available from the U.S. Geological Survey. The map that goes along with the Kious and Tilling book is especially informative.

For further information on marmots, see *Marmots: Social Behavior and Ecology*, by David P. Barash.

Information about Scott Fischer's death on Everest was drawn from a number of secondhand and printed sources, including Claudia Glenn Dowling's August 1996 article in *Life* magazine and Jon Krakauer's outstanding book on the Everest disaster, *Into Thin Air*.

John Muir's summit climb is recounted in *John of the Mountains: The Unpublished Journals of John Muir,* edited by Linnie Marsh Wolfe; and in Aubrey Haines' *Mountain Fever*. Muir's essay "An Ascent of Mount Rainier" is reprinted in his collection *Steep Trails*.

Nontechnical references on high altitude begin with Charles Houston's classic *Going Higher: The Story of Man and Altitude. Medicine for Mountaineering,* edited by James A. Wilkerson, is a good book to keep in camp, if not on the trail. Other useful sources include *High Altitude and Man,* John B. West and Sukhamay Lahiri, editors; *High Altitude Medicine and Physiology*, second edition, Michael P. Ward, et al. Historical material was drawn from *Mediaeval Lore from Bartholomew Anglicus,* by Robert Steele; *The Tarikh-I-Rashidi, or, A History of the Moghuls of Central Asia,* by Mirza Muhammad Haidar, edited by N. Elias, translated by E. Denison Ross; *The Respiratory Function of the Blood, Part I: Lessons from High Altitude*, by Joseph Barcroft; and *Mountain Gloom and Mountain Glory* by Marjorie Hope Nicolson. Hornbein and Messner's high-altitude experiences come from *Everest: The West Ridge,* by Thomas Hornbein; and *The Crystal Horizon,* by Reinhold Messner. Many of the studies cited in this chapter come from medical journal articles too numerous to cite; interested readers may write to the publisher and request the list.

Cascade-Olympic Natural History: A Trailside Reference, by Daniel Mathews, is a wonderfully literate and comprehensive trail companion; I relied upon Mathews's knowledge and spent many mountain evenings with his elegant prose. Other sources included *Mountain Plants of the Pacific Northwest*, by Ronald J. Taylor and George W. Douglas; *Mountain Flowers of the Cascades & Olympics*, by Harvey Manning; *Wildflowers of Mount Rainier and the Cascades*, by Mary A. Fries; *Western Forests*, by Stephen Whitney; and *Northwest Trees*, by Stephen F. Arno and Ramona P. Hammerly. Among the sources for specific botanic research were "The Role of Lupine in Succession on Mount St. Helens," by William F. Morris and David M. Wood, *Ecology*, June 1989; "Mending the Meadow: High-Altitude Meadow Restoration in Mount Rainier National Park," by Regina M. Rochefort and Stephen T. Gibbons, *Restoration & Management Notes*, Winter 1992; and "Temporal and Spatial Distribution of Trees in Subalpine Meadows of Mount Rainier National Park, Washington, U.S.A.," by Regina M. Rochefort and David L. Peterson, *Arctic and Alpine Research*, 1996 (volume 28, number 1). For information about the Park Service's tenure at Mount Rainier, see *Wonderland: An Administrative History of Mount Rainier National Park*, by Theodore Catton, available at the National Park Service library in Seattle.

The story of the Marine transport disaster was culled from interviews, newspaper reports, and National Park Service records stored in the National Archives' Pacific Northwest regional repository in Seattle. The deaths of Sean Ryan and Phil Otis were reported from interviews and the official National Park Service Case Record, with additional material from Melanie Mavrides's August 20, 1995, *New York Times* story and Hal Clifford's article, "Tragedy on Mount Rainier," in *Snow Country*, January 1996.

Marjorie Hope Nicolson's brilliant book on the cultural, religious, literary, and historical meanings of mountains, *Mountain Gloom and*

Mountain Glory, was recently reprinted by the University of Washington Press. My research was aided by *Early Travellers in the Alps*, by Gavin R. De Beer; *The European Witch-Craze of the Sixteenth and Seventeenth Centuries*, by H. R. Trevor-Roper; *The Sacred Mountain of Tibet: On Pilgrimage to Kailas*, by Russell Johnson and Kerry Moran; *Images and Symbols*, by Mircea Eliade; *Cuchama and Sacred Mountains*, by W. Y. Evans-Wentz; *Dawn Behind the Dawn: A Search for an Earthly Paradise,* by Geoffrey Ashe; *The Idea of the Holy*, by Rudolf Otto; and "Ascending Mount Fuji," by T. R. Reid, in the August 27, 1994, *Washington Post*.

Accounts of both the Kautz and the Stevens/Van Trump ascents can be found in Meany's *Mount Rainier: A Record of Exploration*. Fred Beckey's *Cascade Alpine Guide 1* contains the most accurate route information for climbers considering Rainier.

INDEX

Page numbers in boldface indicate map

A–B